Friedrich Lippmann

Drawings by Sandro Botticelli for Dante's Divina Commedia

Reduced facsimiles after the originals in the Royal Museum, Berlin, and in the Vatican Library

Friedrich Lippmann

Drawings by Sandro Botticelli for Dante's Divina Commedia
Reduced facsimiles after the originals in the Royal Museum, Berlin, and in the Vatican Library

ISBN/EAN: 9783337246099

Printed in Europe, USA, Canada, Australia, Japan

Cover: Foto ©Thomas Meinert / pixelio.de

More available books at **www.hansebooks.com**

DRAWINGS

BY

SANDRO BOTTICELLI

FOR

DANTE'S DIVINA COMMEDIA

DRAWINGS BY SANDRO BOTTICELLI FOR DANTE'S DIVINA COMMEDIA

REDUCED FACSIMILES AFTER THE ORIGINALS IN THE ROYAL MUSEUM BERLIN AND IN THE VATICAN LIBRARY WITH AN INTRODUCTION AND COMMENTARY BY F. LIPPMANN

LONDON. LAWRENCE AND BULLEN

MDCCCXCVI

PRINTED AT THE IMPERIAL PRESS BERLIN

TABLE OF CONTENTS

INTRODUCTION

AMONG those artists of the Italian Renaissance whose pictures make a lasting impression, even on the hastier and less critical visitors to European galleries, Botticelli is one of the most attractive. He does not, indeed, dazzle and entrance by the force and splendour of his genius, the power and majesty of his conceptions, as do Leonardo, Michael Angelo, and Raphael. His charm lies rather in the sweet and delicate play of fancy, the depths of quaint yet sympathetic emotion that make up his artistic personality. When Fra Angelico leads us through the realms of the blessed, he sheds over his figures an ineffable brightness, the holy calm proper to souls freed from the last vestige of earthly trammels; and something of the same radiant detachment from earthly things animates the creations of Botticelli. But whereas with Fra Angelico, art gushes from springs of deep religious feeling, with Botticelli it is always the poet who inspires the painter. This special stamp of individuality is strongly impressed on all his works.

Humanity had lost its grasp on the traditions of antique art, and had ceased to look Nature frankly in the face. But from Giotto to Leonardo, we note a gradual awakening to the truth and power of natural phenomena; the children of the new day turn, timidly at first, once more to the great Mother. This unexampled period of revival is marked by every gift of youth grace, *naïveté*, freshness of sensation, and an elasticity of creative power which no adverse forces from without could repress.

Botticelli was one of the lights, though in no strict sense one of the leaders of the Florentine School. To those qualities which make up the distinctive charm of the *quattrocentisti*, he added an element all his own, the fairy glamour of a dream-world, born of his poetic temperament.

Our knowledge of Botticelli's life is confined to a few meagre facts: his biography, as given by Vasari, is of the scantiest. It is not improbable that in his later years especially he was one of those self-contained beings of whom contemporaries have little to say.

Botticelli, youngest of the five sons of the tanner Mariano di Vanni Filipepi, was born at Florence in 1446. Sandro is an abbreviation of Alessandro, and the surname Botticelli—Botticello, literally, the little cask—was formerly explained as resulting from the artist's apprenticeship to a certain goldsmith distinguished by this sobriquet. But it appears that Sandro's eldest brother, a broker, was also called Botticelli by his friends, and that the name was afterwards transferred to the painter. In the only specimen of his signature now extant, however, he writes himself: Sandro di Mariano.

Vasari tells us that the young Mariano was very carefully brought up, and instructed in the branches of learning usually taught to the boys of his times. Although he shewed a ready comprehension of things which appealed to his tastes, he seems to have had little aptitude for the drudgery of reading, writing, and arithmetic. His father, impatient with the vagaries of the strange youth, removed him from school, and apprenticed him to his godfather, a goldsmith of repute. Either Vasari's account of his youthful idleness was false, or Botticelli must have diligently atoned for his early shortcomings, for we know him to have been deeply versed in classic literature, and a student of Dante, while his handwriting is almost that of a professor of learning.

In those days many branches of the fine arts were practised side by side in the goldsmith's workshop. The workers in precious metals were actively allied to the painters, and artists such as Pollajuolo wielded the goldsmith's hammer and plied the brush by turns. The casting of metals, sculpture, intaglio, and artistic needlework, were carried on in the same ateliers, and Sandro, who shewed much aptitude in his new calling, devoted himself more especially to painting and drawing.

Yielding to his son's desire, the tanner accordingly placed the youth with the Carmelite friar Filippo Lippi, one of the most renowned masters of the day. But Botticelli's early apprenticeship to the goldsmith was not without its effect on his work as a painter. His skill in the rendering of ornaments and decorative accessories, and his evident delight in their treatment are no doubt traceable to these early influences, as may well be also the sharpness and decision of outline that characterize his drawing.

Botticelli probably became Fra Filippo's pupil about 1460. Born about 1406, and brought up in the Carmelite monastery at Florence, Filippo's artistic development owed much to the genius of Masaccio. In emulation of his great prototype, he strove earnestly to breathe into the hieratic convention of religious painting the new spirit of truth and beauty. Filippo, in spite of his devout calling, had all the unbridled fervour of the artistic temperament. His genius was sullied by moral weaknesses, which it is only fair to judge by the standard of his own times. In 1452 he quitted Florence for the neighbouring town of Prato, where he was employed in the frescoes of the cathedral choir. In 1466 he removed to Spoleto, and settling there, undertook a vast scheme of decoration in the Duomo, a commission procured for him by his patron Piero de' Medici. He died at Spoleto in 1469. It was at Prato that he seduced from her vows the fair Lucretia Buti, a nun of the convent of which he was chaplain. He afterwards married her, the necessary dispensation being granted by Pope Pius II. who released both parties from their religious obligations. Of this union was born Filippino Lippi, the pupil of Botticelli, an artist hardly less famous than his father and his master.

In Fra Filippo's compositions, which generally contain numerous figures, a certain artistic equilibrium takes the place of real freedom and spontaneous balance in arrangement. Many of his heads and figures have a curiously flattened appearance, as if pressure from above had increased their width. On the other hand, he has bequeathed to us creations of such joyous actuality, grace, and delicacy as the *Annunciation* in the National Gallery of London, the *Madonna with the Infant Christ and two Angels* in the Uffizi, and the *Birth of Christ* in the Berlin Gallery. His angels and Madonnas have a peculiar sweetness and purity of expression, a delicate proportion of form, a dewy softness of flesh-tones. In his finest works, the colour is rich, brilliant, and glowing.

Botticelli's apprenticeship to Filippo came to an end, no doubt, before the latter settled at Spoleto in 1466. At Filippo's death, two years later, Botticelli was recognized as one of the best painters in Florence, and as an artist of the highest rank.

Vasari mentions the allegorical figure of *Fortitude* executed for the hall of the Mercatanzia in Florence, and now in the Uffizi, as one of his earliest independent works. Antonio and Piero del Pollajuolo had painted six other *Virtues* for the same place. Earlier works are mentioned, which have not come down to us, notably the portraits of the leaders of the Pazzi conspiracy, and the murderers of Giuliano de' Medici (1478), which Botticelli, in accordance with a stern custom of the day, painted as a memorial of infamy on the walls of the Palazzo Pubblico. The paintings he executed jointly with Domenico Ghirlandajo in the Sala della Udienza of the same building have also perished.

None of Botticelli's known works bear either date or signature, and only in a few instances are we able to assign them with any confidence to a particular period. We can therefore only approximately trace the course of his artistic development. Further difficulties beset us from the fact that Botticelli early surrounded himself with a numerous band of pupils and assistants. In his *bottega*, a combination of school and workshop such as grew up round every popular master of the times, pictures were executed, for the more important parts of which, such as the heads and hands, the master was himself responsible, while the rest was left to his assistants. They were also employed in replicas and copies, or in the execution of works for which he furnished the designs. All such works bear the impress, more or less modified, of Botticelli's peculiar character. But if we wish to enjoy in full measure the charm of his art, we must distinguish between these and works entirely by his own hand. In some cases, of course, this process of discrimination presents difficulties.

That Botticelli's most striking characteristics, both as draughtsman and colourist, were fairly pronounced even when he first quitted Fra Filippo's atelier, the *Fortezza* already mentioned bears witness. Side by side with the influence of Lippi, so clearly traceable in his work, that of the Florentine sculptor and painter Verrocchio is also apparent, and it has been conjectured that he worked for a time under the latter, after leaving his first master.

Botticelli is perhaps most readily distinguished from Fra Filippo by the greater spirituality of expression in his Madonnas and angels. These have a distinct and very striking individuality, apart from any high standard of ideal beauty. The facial type is peculiar; the bony substructure of the heads is very strongly indicated, the check bones are prominent; the noses have a slight inward curve, and a tendency to thickness towards the end, the eyelids are heavy and sleepy, the mouths full and richly curved, the chins firm and strongly marked. His angels have slightly hollow cheeks, and a delicate, almost suffering expression of dreamy longing and melancholy. Like his feminine figures, they are full of a sweet fascination, and their rapt, soulful gaze stamps itself ineffaceably on the mind of the spectator.

Botticelli had an intimate knowledge of human anatomy, as we see even in such an early work as the life-size *Saint Sebastian* in the Berlin Gallery. Unlike many of his contemporaries, however, he concerned himself less with the human form as an object for learned anatomical demonstration and detail, than as a medium for the expression of character and feeling. Herein lies the secret of his success as a delineator of noble and rhythmic movement, and to this tendency we owe no doubt, much of that peculiarly individual grace which distinguishes his floating angels and his dancing maidens. The flow of his lines is aided and enhanced by a free, yet carefully considered cast of draperies, inspired to some extent by classic models, though modified by personal fancy. In some cases we find these draperies clinging in close folds about the limbs, in others fluttering loosely in the breeze.

Throughout his best works, the colour is uniformly bright and high in tone, yet powerful and full of a soft inward glow. The local tints are very clearly defined, producing a sort of gem-like effect, which is enhanced by the occasional use of gold leaf, a practice of the early masters often resorted to by Botticelli. We have already spoken of his refined treatment of ornamental accessories; he was also fond of introducing garlands of foliage, thickets, and hedges of flowers, or leaves and branches decoratively treated, by way of background to his subjects. Leonardo's assertion, that Botticelli was incapable of painting a landscape, had its justification from the Leonardesque standpoint. Even when he introduced a landscape background, he treated it as a mere accessory, and subordinated it entirely to the development of his figures, and their characterization.

Throughout his later period of activity, Botticelli diverged more and more from the old severe and hieratic conception of the Virgin, the influence of which is very apparent in his early works. Fra Filippo had indeed, already treated groups of the Madonna with the Holy Child and the little St. John as purely human scenes of family life. But to this modern rendering of the sacred theme, Botticelli added an element of his own, the expression of a deep mystic relation between the Mother and Child. With the maternal joy of his Madonna is mingled a soft melancholy, a premonition of the sufferings in store for the Babe. And this brooding spirit seems to have communicated itself to the Child, who gazes out upon the world as if lost in nascent thought.

A hitherto unknown form of Madonna picture came into vogue in the time of Botticelli. This was the circular panel, called by the Italians a *tondo*. As it had never been used by the early ecclesiastical painters, there was no recognized type proper to this form of composition, and the artist's creative genius had consequently more scope than in the treatment of the usual square, upright, or oblong panel. Genre passages, such as pleased the taste of the day, could be introduced in the *tondi* without any violation of tradition. No painter of the Renaissance made a more consummate use of this new artistic departure than Botticelli. The most famous of his circular pictures is the Virgin writing the Magnificat, with attendant angels, in the Uffizi. The circular line which enframes the composition is echoed by the bending figures of the angels; the painter seems to be holding up for our contemplation a magic mirror, in which we see reflected an apparition from a higher world. Among the several round pictures closely allied to this Florentine example, we may mention those in the London National Gallery and the Turin Museum.

Botticelli's angels are the creatures of his own poetic fancy, beings cast in a human mould, of a very individual type, their angelic nature indicated chiefly by their sexlessness. They might be either youths or maidens, and this uncertainty is deliberate on the painter's part. It betokens no want of capacity for the rendering of distinctive types, for, as many examples of his art attest, he was a most accomplished portrait-painter. The male portraits in the Louvre, in the Berlin Museum and in the Liechtenstein Gallery, and the portrait of a woman, formerly the property of Dante Rossetti, and now in Mr. Constantine Ionides' collection, are instinct with truth, vitality, and animation of the highest order. This side of Botticelli's art is finely displayed in the numerous figures of his *Adoration of the Kings* in the Uffizi, a large composition of the most striking originality. Diverging widely from the conventional treatment of the theme, it is a bold and comprehensive attempt to connect sacred legend and contemporary history. The worshipping Magi and their followers are members of the house of Medici, or of persons closely allied to that house, some among them still living when the picture was painted, others dead. Close to the Virgin kneels Cosimo, the Father of his Country (d. 1464): a little beyond him Giuliano de' Medici, Lorenzo the Magnificent, Filippo Strozzi, Andrea Poliziano and others, whose types are more or less easily recognizable from existing coins, medals, and busts. In the extreme corner to the right stands a man in a long yellow robe, looking out at the spectator. His face, with its powerful, somewhat heavy features, and thoughtful expression, is reproduced in the vignette at the beginning of this volume. It is a portrait of Botticelli, who here introduces himself in the character of an adherent of the Medici, his patrons.

It was characteristic of the Renaissance spirit to feel no incongruity in the blending of the sacred and the profane. Botticelli's *Adoration of the Kings* is, in fact, a portrait-group of the Medici. Pagan and Christian symbols are unhesitatingly introduced side by side. Once more, as in the classic ages, art sought to awaken the religious sentiment of the spectator, by an appeal to the higher sensuous faculties, and it was by virtue of his reliance upon this appeal that Botticelli became the *choragus* of the modern movement. In the *Coronation of the Virgin*, at the Florentine Academy, the group of God the Father and the Madonna is surrounded by a circle of dancing angels, strewing flowers, a joyous celestial band, marked by the most lively animation and sense of movement. Each one of these angels, whose affinity to the Hours and Graces of antique art the master was at no pains to disguise, shews a distinctive individuality, both in facial type, and in the freely harmonized colours of his fluttering draperies. St. Ambrose and St. Jerome, who with the two other Fathers, stand below, turn an astonished gaze heavenwards. The conception is more severe in the picture of the Madonna with the two Saints in the Berlin Gallery. Here the painter, debarred by the nature of his subject from the freedom and animation proper to him, has supplied their place by the splendour of the accessories among which he has placed his figures. A mass of luxuriant vegetation, tastefully interwoven in a trellis, forms a background for the richly decorated throne of the Virgin.

Antique art and antique literature were the springs from which the Italian painters and sculptors of the fifteenth century drew both form and idea. Antiquity lay, as yet, hidden behind a mysterious veil, lifted at intervals by the breeze, and affording only glimpses of the great secrets to be revealed. Artists knew enough to incite them to new aims, but not enough to paralyze their own inventive gifts, and throw them off the track of original development. The simplicity and freshness with which they invest antique motives and materials, give the charm and aroma of a fairy legend to their rendering of classic subjects. Botticelli determined the treatment of such material throughout the middle ages to a far greater degree than Mantegna, with his more pronounced archæological tendencies. The few works in this new genre which have come down to us constitute one of the various titles to fame both of Botticelli's art and of the Florentine School. Foremost among them is the large picture in the Academy at Florence, generally known as "Spring", which, however, is taken from a description in Politian's poem "Giostra", and is, in fact, an allegory of the realm of Venus. Giuliano de' Medici, the hero of this epic, is represented as a wanderer in the Cytherean fields, the goddess herself appearing as the central figure of the composition. Cupid hovers over the three Graces, shooting fiery arrows from his bow; Flora, Zephyr, and the Goddess of Spring advance from the opposite side. A luxuriant carpet of flowers and verdure decks the ground of the orange grove in which the scene is laid.

Another passage of Politian's poem inspired the *Birth of Venus* in the Uffizi. Both pictures were originally in Cosimo I.'s Villa, Castello. Less attractive than these is a kindred work, also in the Uffizi, the so-called *Calumny of Apelles*, a subject from Lucian often treated by artists of the fifteenth and sixteenth centuries, and necessitating a certain dry didactic treatment which fettered the free play of the artist's fancy, though individual passages are carefully and sympathetically carried out.

From 1481 to 1483 Botticelli was in Rome, where he painted two large frescoes on the south wall of the Sistine Chapel. Pope Sixtus IV. had invited him to decorate the newly completed building, in conjunction with Ghirlandajo, Signorelli, Cosimo Rosselli and Pinturicchio. One of Botticelli's frescoes represents the deeds of Moses in the land of Midian; the other, according to the latest interpretation, *The Sacrifice of Cleansing after Leprosy*, with the *Temptation of Christ* in the background. The modern visitor to the Sistine Chapel is, as a rule, so dazzled by Michael Angelo's stupendous works in the vault and choir, that he does less than justice to the compositions of earlier masters. But even when we consider these separately and with due attention, we cannot but admit that Botticelli's finest qualities fall short of their highest development here, in spite of many passages of great beauty. The vast scale in which he was compelled to work, the nature of the subject, and the obligation laid upon him to bring together a number of distinct episodes within the space of a single composition, were alike uncongenial to the peculiar bent of his genius. Filippino Lippi, the son of Fra Filippo, worked as his assistant on the *Temptation of Christ*.

Of Botticelli's other works in fresco, few have survived, but these sufficiently prove that when working with a free hand on suitable material, he was no less original and effective in this genre than as a painter of easel pictures. We may instance the little wall painting of St. Jerome in his study, in the Ognissanti at Florence, and the fragments of frescoes from the Villa Lemmi, near Florence, representing Lorenzo Tornabuoni introduced into the circle of the arts and sciences, and his wife Giovanna receiving gifts from Venus and the Graces. These fragments, now in the Louvre, suffice at least to shew that the frescoes must have been among the most brilliant creations of the artist's fancy.

From 1480 to about 1494 was perhaps the most prolific period of Botticelli's activity. He was then the head of a large atelier in Florence, where innumerable *bottega* pictures and replicas of his works were produced. To this period also, in all probability, must be referred his close study of Dante, and the execution of the greater part of the drawings illustrating the Divine Comedy. Before dealing with these, however, we propose to complete our sketch of the artist's career.

As far as it is possible to judge from the somewhat scanty historical details now extant, Botticelli's life seems to have been singularly calm and equable. The large following of pupils and assistants he is known to have had, and the landed property he owned in Florence, point to the conclusion that he was in easy circumstances. Nor did he lack his due meed of credit and consideration among his fellow-citizens. He belonged to that band of artists, poets, and men of letters whom the Medici, then the virtual kings and rulers of Florence, had attracted to their court. In 1491, when it was determined to build a new façade to the Duomo, the most distinguished artists in Italy were invited to judge of the plans, and among them we find Botticelli.

The advent of Savonarola made a deep impression on him, which manifests itself in all his later works. The Ferrarese monk, who believed himself especially called to wage a divinely ordained war upon the vices of the age, and the crimes of the church, came to the Florentine Convent of San Marco in 1482. It was not, however, until 1490 that Savonarola's extraordinary influence over the popular mind fully manifested itself. His Lenten sermons attracted thousands. When his reiterated prophecies of the impending downfall of the Medici were apparently fulfilled by the entry of Charles VIII. into Florence, and the deposition of the shifty Piero de' Medici, the Florentines hailed him as a God-appointed seer. Savonarola became a sort of theocratic sovereign of the city. So great was the number of his would-be disciples that the convent of San Marco had to be enlarged. His dream was to send forth from Florence a voice that should recall the world to virtue and the fear of God. He preached against luxury and self-indulgence, enjoining an immediate return to simplicity and chastity as the sole means of salvation. Novel *autos-da-fé* were inaugurated, and the converted Florentines hastened to the burning piles to cast into the flames magnificent apparel, costly plate, worldly books, playing cards, and all such pictures as were supposed to appeal to the sensual instincts. Many a priceless masterpiece was no doubt sacrificed to the blind fanaticism of the moment. Savonarola was by no means hostile to art: but he insisted that it should find only such expression as tended to the purification and religious advancement of mankind.

Fra Angelico's frescoes in San Marco were to him as heavenly melodies. He desired to see the spirit of devotion breathing forth from the painter's creations: no profane thought was to find utterance in such works: the very features of saints and angels were to be drawn from the artist's spiritual vision, not suggested by persons with whom they were familiar, far less deliberately reproduced, so as to be in fact contemporary portraits. No longer was it to be possible for the Florentines to say, as they had been in the habit of doing: Behold a Magdalen, or: Such an one might be the Blessed Mother herself! The dress and accessories of the Virgin were to be as plain and simple as possible. Pictures, he contended, should not be a source of material enjoyment, a mere satisfaction of the eye. He urged repeatedly upon his hearers a maxim often formulated by mediaeval asceticism—that the sole function of pictures in churches was to bring home the truths of salvation to the minds of the ignorant and unlearned.

Savonarola's influence threatened for a time to curb and restrain even the fully developed artistic life of Florence. Material interests and the new-born spirit of delight in life at last combined in energetic resistance to his onslaught.

Foremost among his opponents was the Guild of brocade-weavers. The warring factions were distinguished by nick-names, the adherents of the new prophet being called the *Piangioni* (The Weepers), his enemies the *Arrabiati* (The Infuriated). These events were not without their influence upon Botticelli. From the character of his art we divine in him a naturally sensitive, somewhat enthusiastic disposition, tempered by a strain of gentle melancholy, and a leaning towards mysticism which his absorbing study of Dante may well have fostered. Botticelli became an adherent of Savonarola's, and after his conversion by the inspired monk, he seems to have looked upon the earlier manifestations of his genius as culpable lapses, and never to have returned to the full and unfettered play of his natural fancy. We know not whether Savonarola's excommunication by the Pope, and his tragic death at the stake

(May 23rd, 1498) tended to alienate the convert from his teacher. The few pictures painted at this period betray the sorrowful preoccupations of the master, not only in the choice of subject, but in the noticeable "degradation" of tone and tints, to be observed, for instance, in the *Entombment* of the Munich Pinacothek, and the smaller version of the same theme in the Poldi Pezzoli collection at Milan. A like sense of melancholy, though here of a more poetic and less sombre cast, pervades the *Nativity* of the London National Gallery. The picture bears the date 1500, and a long Greek inscription on the upper edge refers to the prophecies of the Apocalypse, and recognizes their partial fulfilment in recent calamities in Italy. The new-born Saviour lies in the centre, the Virgin kneeling in adoration. Pilgrims arriving on the scene are greeted by angels, who embrace them with an energetic display of passionate emotion, while above, other angels, singing and dancing in ecstacy, float heavenward bearing the glad tidings. The spectators of the scene wear a calm and peaceful expression as of satisfied yearning: the reconciliation between God and man is complete.

This is the latest work by Botticelli known to us. In 1503, he, and several other veterans gave judgment as to the most suitable site for Michael Angelo's *David*. After this, we find no further details of his life, beyond the general statement that his last years were spent in suffering and solitude, from which death released him on May 17th, 1510. The family vault of the Filipepi in the Ognissanti at Florence enshrines the dust of that master who first among the moderns gave back to art the vanished delight of the antique world in the rendering of human grace and loveliness.

Certain portions of the Divine Comedy were well-known throughout Italy in Dante's life-time, and after his death (1321), the whole poem was repeatedly copied, and widely circulated. Manuscripts for rich amateurs were generally written on parchment by skilled calligraphists, the initial letters of cantos and divisions being, as was usual in mediaeval codices, illuminated in gold and colours. In many instances, an ornamentation springing from the initial, extended over the whole page. Within the opening letter of the poem, it was customary to enclose a portrait of Dante, writing, in which the artist made a more or less successful attempt at likeness, or a group of Dante and Virgil, or a miniature presentment of some familiar episode. In the more costly manuscripts, illuminations occupying half, or sometimes the whole of a page were introduced, on which the painter bestowed his utmost care and skill in the delineation of some characteristic scene from the canto before him.

Occasionally, calligraphy and illumination were the work of one hand; but a special class of painters, the miniaturists, who devoted themselves exclusively to the illumination of manuscripts, were generally employed on these decorations. The artistic value of their work is, as a rule, very slight. Dante introduces one of the masters of this craft, Oderisi of Gubbio, in the eleventh canto of the Purgatory (V. 79 et seq.). Recognizing the painter, he thus addresses him:

"Art thou not Oderisi? art not thou
Agobbio's glory, glory of that art
Which they of Paris call the limner's skill?"

Even after the introduction of printing in Italy, manuscript copies of the Divine Comedy continued to be produced, though the new art developed rapidly during the last years of the fifteenth century. Between 1472, when Dante's poem was printed for the first time, and 1500, some eighteen editions of the Divine Comedy were published in Italy. But printed books were at first looked upon as mere cheap substitutes for manuscripts. Wealthy collectors despised them, as they loved to see their favourite authors in a costly dress. A contemporary biographer of

Duke Federigo of Urbino writes as follows: "Every book in the ducal library is of faultless beauty, written by hand on parchment, and adorned with miniatures. There is not a single printed book in the collection. The Duke would have been ashamed to own any such". Nevertheless transcribers and illuminators found it hard to hold their own against the printers. By the elaborate ornamentation of their texts they endeavoured to secure to themselves a field in which they were safe from the competition of the latter. This explains the production of so many of the most magnificent Italian manuscripts in the last years of the fifteenth century, at a time when the ultimate victory of printer over scribe was already assured.

The written edition of the Divine Comedy illustrated by Botticelli's drawings was evidently designed on the plan of those costly manuscripts usually decorated by the miniaturists. But rising immeasurably above all kindred works, it became one of the most significant artistic renderings ever given to poetry, and not the least among the many marvels of the Italian Renaissance.

In a series of notes upon Florentine artists "from Cimabue to Michelangelo" collected by some unknown writer of the sixteenth century, we find the following reference to Botticelli: "he painted and illustrated a Dante on parchment for Lorenzo di Pier Francesco de' Medici, which was accounted a most marvellous work" ("Dipinse et storio un Dante incartapecora alorenzo di piero francesco de' Medici il che fu cosa maravigliosa tenuto". See MS. in the National Library at Florence. Cf. also Vasari (Milanesi) III, p. 317, note †). The Lorenzo here mentioned was a son of Pier Francesco de' Medici, born about 1456. He played no prominent part in the affairs of his day, but he seems to have been a lover of the arts, for we know that Michelangelo received a commission from him for a statue of a youthful John the Baptist. He died in 1503.

Of Botticelli's preoccupation with the works of Dante we glean something from Vasari, who tells us, that after completing his frescoes in the Sistine Chapel, the artist returned in all haste to Florence, where "his speculative mind found a congenial task in annotating a portion of Dante; he also illustrated the Inferno, and caused it to be printed. In these pursuits much time was spent, and as he neglected his work for them, many complications arose in his affairs". This, though in itself somewhat perplexing, is explained and confirmed as to the main fact by our later and more complete knowledge, and by the note of the anonymous Florentine above mentioned. That Botticelli wrote a commentary on any part of Dante's poem is hardly credible, but this statement seems to have been an error arising out of the painter's absorbing interest in the poet's works.

The Dante illustrated by Botticelli for Lorenzo di Pierfrancesco disappeared and was entirely forgotten until the present century. The first to call attention to it in modern times was G. F. Waagen. He saw the volume with the drawings in the Duke of Hamilton's collection at Hamilton Palace, and recognized the work as that of Botticelli, though he was of opinion that a few of the illustrations might have been by some other artist. He called to mind the passage we have quoted from Vasari, and unhesitatingly pronounced the drawings the finest ever executed in illustration of the Divine Comedy (Treasures of Art, III, p. 307). But it was not until the volume passed into the Berlin Museum in 1882, with other manuscripts from the Hamilton Collection, that the drawings became widely known, or that Botticelli was finally recognized as their sole author. The series consists of eighty-eight sheets of parchment, eighty-five of which are illustrated. They average about 12 inches in height by 14 in width, and were bound together in boards, apparently in the eighteenth century, when the book was also furnished with an index by one Claudio Molini, an Italian bookseller in Paris. From this we find that the number of drawings has been preserved intact since his time.

Soon after the acquisition of the volume by the Berlin Museum, it was discovered that there were eight drawings belonging to the same series in the Vatican Library, on seven sheets of parchment. These sheets, bound together in a thin volume, originally belonged to Queen Christina of Sweden, who died at Rome in 1689, when her library, or the principal part of it, was bought by Pope Alexander VIII, and incorporated with that of the Vatican. When these eight drawings were separated from the rest is not known. Colomb de Batines mentions them in his Bibliografia Dantesca (Prato, 1856, II, p. 174, no. 331). He was struck by their remarkable drawing and rich composition, but expresses no opinion as to their authorship. The Vatican drawings are: the introductory plan or chart of Hell, the illustration to Canto I (these are drawn on either side of the same sheet); and the illustrations to Cantos IX,

X, XII, XIII, XV and XVI of the Inferno; the drawing for Canto VIII is at Berlin. From Canto XVII of the Inferno to Canto XXX of the Paradiso the Berlin drawings continue in an unbroken series. The page on which the illustration to Canto XXXI should have appeared, is blank, and the series closes with the unfinished drawing for Canto XXXII.

The sheets on which the drawings are made, are of fine goatskin parchment averaging $12^1/_2$ inches high by $18^1/_2$ wide. On the smooth, or so-called "fleshy side" are the drawings, on the rough or "hairy side" of each sheet, a canto of the poem, divided into six columns, and written in a character known in Italy as "Alla Antica". The original arrangement of the sheets was such that the text to each illustration faced it, so that the reader, on opening the book, had both drawing and poem before him. The text was written before the artist began his drawings, but the large initials are omitted, a space being left for these at the beginning of each canto. We give a specimen of the calligraphy (from Inferno XXX, V. 74-81).

Come adscaldar sappoggia teghia ategghia.
Dalcapo alpie dischianze macolati.
E enon udi gia mai menare streghia.
Adragazo adspectato dalsignor so
Ne da colui che mal uolentier ueghia
C eme ciascun menaua spesso ilmorso.
Dellunghie sopra se per la gran rabbia
Del pizicor che non ha piu soccorso.

All the drawings are sketched in with a soft silver-point, probably composed of an alloy of silver and lead, and finished with the pen in black or brown ink: the lightly touched outlines are shaded here and there where modelling is to be suggested. Two of the Vatican sheets, the plan of Hell, and the drawing for Inferno XV, and one of the Berlin drawings, that belonging to Inferno XVIII, are gaily painted in body-colour; in a third Vatican illustration, that of Inferno X, only the dresses of some of the figures are coloured.

Not only does the general character of these drawings at once suggest Botticelli, but a careful study of their details confirms the belief that they were entirely executed by him. We recognize throughout the specific character of his art as manifested in his best pictures, the peculiar sense of movement, the type of head, the somewhat melancholy and suffering expression of the features, the full lips, the slight inward curve of the nose, and the rich folds of floating draperies. In the drawing to the twenty-eighth canto of the Paradiso, representing the nine angelic circles, the angels in the lowest circle hold small tablets in their hands. On one of these is inscribed in minute but perfectly legible characters: Sandro di Mariano. It is probable that Botticelli did not intend this actually as a signature, for the tiny letters might easily be overlooked; the inscription perhaps only expressed the master's pious wish that his name might not be forgotten in the beatific circle. The character and the ink used for the inscription are identical with those of the quotations under several of the drawings, obviously written by the artist himself. We give an enlarged reproduction of the cartellino.

Are these drawings finished compositions or mere sketches? This question cannot fail to suggest itself to the student. Many manuscripts of the fifteenth century and of an earlier date, among them some of the Divine Comedy itself, are illustrated with outline drawings. It is quite possible therefore, that Botticelli may have contemplated this style of treatment. On the other hand, the illuminated drawings in the Inferno shew that it was at first proposed to colour the illustrations, and that the attempt was made, perhaps at the wish of the patron. It was then, no doubt, decided that colouring was unsuitable, and the idea was abandoned. The master's final intention was, probably, to give his drawings their present character, that of a cycle of artistic sketches.

A further question has been raised as to whether Botticelli himself coloured the sheets, or whether this was done by some professional illuminator. The works of the Italian miniaturists of that period are distinguished by great delicacy of execution and brilliance of tone. But in the Dante drawings the colour is dull and sombre, the general effect unpleasant and wanting in harmony. These very defects point to the conclusion, that Botticelli himself laid on the colours. Unversed in the technique of painting upon parchment, he was unable to obtain a satisfactory result with his materials. A practised miniaturist would have handled them differently, and no doubt more successfully.

Each canto is illustrated by a single drawing, with the exception of Canto XXXIV of the Inferno, where two drawings are devoted to the presentment of the gigantic Lucifer, the first a half, the second a full-length figure, extending over two opposite pages.

Throughout the Inferno and Purgatorio, almost every pictorial motive in the narrative is treated by the artist. In his illustrations of the text, he does not confine himself to the incidents of a single canto, but occasionally introduces episodes from the close of the preceding, or the beginning of the following section. When several scenes are depicted in one drawing, they appear side by side without any definite limitation of the action, and hence we find the figures of Dante and Virgil, or those of the poet's later guides or companions appearing twice, or occasionally several times in a single illustration. This method of composition, in accordance with which the events of successive periods were depicted within the limits of a single pictorial plane, the various groups distinct one from another, but each naïvely repeating the chief figures in the drama, was universal in early art, and Botticelli adopted it in his frescoes in the Sistine Chapel, as well as in the Dante drawings. The modern principle of unity of action within the limits of a single composition gained ground but slowly in the fifteenth century. Nevertheless, the numerous figures introduced in the illustrations to the Inferno and Purgatorio are clearly differentiated. The movements and, in many cases, the complicated attitudes of the nude forms are firmly rendered, and the artist shews a complete grasp of physiognomy, and of individual character as expressed in physical structure.

In the Inferno and Purgatorio the compositions contain a great variety of small figures, whereas in the Paradiso the scale is larger, and in many of the drawings, Dante and Beatrice appear alone.

It is interesting to note how Botticelli, in spite of the freedom with which he approached his task, occasionally retains the types laid down by former illustrators. Our two reproductions, one an outline drawing of the griffin in the Purgatorio, from a manuscript of the second half of the fourteenth century*, the other the fettered giants of the Inferno from a somewhat later codex, may serve to illustrate this connection between the artist and his predecessors.

* This Dante manuscript is in the library of the Christianeum at Altona. It contains a series of pen-drawings of considerable artistic value; those illustrating the Inferno, and the first twenty-eight cantos of the Purgatorio are somewhat coarsely coloured. The delicate outline drawings of Cantos XXIX to XXXI have been left untouched by the illuminator, as shewn in our reproduction. The series ends abruptly at Canto XXXI of the Purgatorio.

In all probability, Botticelli's designs were produced in the order suggested by the poem. It is evident that the artist gradually attained to a freer and grander conception of his author, and that some episodes appealed to him more than others.

In several of the drawings, the outline of the silver-point has been carefully gone over with the pen in black or brown Indian ink, a notable instance of such treatment being the illustration to Canto X of the Purgatorio, introducing the "Justice of Trajan". Sometimes the first sketch is only gone over in parts, sometimes it is left untouched, and occasionally

Illustration to Canto XXIX of the Purgatorio. From a Dante Manuscript of the XIV century at Altona

Botticelli does not get beyond the preliminaries of a composition. In the illustration to Canto XXXII of the Purgatory, the work advanced no farther than the conception of the three little figures standing by the mystic rose of Paradise, and the illustrations for the two last cantos of the poem were never even begun.

Botticelli is the first, and perhaps the only artist whose pictorial conception of the Divine Comedy does not fall short of the poetical significance. The images of the poet's fancy differed no doubt widely from those by which the artist rendered them, for in every line his work reflects the spirit of the fifteenth century. But Dante's poem has this in common with the Bible, that it lends itself to the forms of expression of every style and period. The very slightness of outline and delicacy of execution adopted by Botticelli enabled him at once to direct the imagination of the spectator and to allow it free play.

The perceptible deepening of spiritual intensity in the compositions as they follow the narrative seems to indicate that they were not all executed at once, but that in spite of the sketchy character of individual drawings Botticelli lingered over them for a considerable time. The passage before quoted from Vasari strengthens this assumption. An unmistakable artistic evolution is accomplished during the progress of the work. We do not know how long a time he spent on them, but it is very possible that these illustrations, undertaken at first perhaps as a relaxation from more arduous labours, gradually enthralled him to such an extent, that his other work was neglected. Such, in fact, may be the meaning of Vasari's statement.

It is very probable that Botticelli began the Dante drawings before he went to Rome in 1481. Vasari says that "he illustrated the Inferno, and caused it to be printed". Now we do possess an edition of the Divine Comedy, printed in Florence in 1481, in which the Inferno is illustrated with nineteen little engravings. The affinity between these plates and Botticelli's drawings is unmistakable. This edition, published under the direction of Cristophoro Landino, and furnished with his commentary on the poem*, it was originally proposed to illustrate with engravings throughout. The plates were to appear as vignettes at the beginning of every canto, although, as a fact, they are only introduced in the first nineteen cantos of the Inferno. Canto III was provided with two vignettes, so that the number of the designs amounts in all to twenty. Throughout the rest of the poem, spaces were left at the head of each canto for the proposed plates**. The engraver has been supposed, on

* As is the case in the majority of the printed works of this period, there is no actual title. Page 1 begins thus: Comento di Christophoro Landino Fiorentino Sopra La Comedia di Dante Alighieri Poeta Fiorentino. The printer's address comes at the end: Impresso in Firenze Per Nicholo di Lorenzo Della Magna A. Di. XXX. Dagosto MD. CCCC. LXXXI. Nicolo della Magna (dell' Allemagna) is the Italianized name of a printer from Breslau, Nikolaus Lorenz.

** Only a few copies of the Dante of 1481, however, contain the plates to all the nineteen cantos. In the greater number, only the first and second cantos are illustrated: other copies are entirely without illustrations, this being the case even in the fine presentation copy on vellum given by Landino to the Signoria of Florence, and now preserved in the National Library of that city.

the authority of a passage in Vasari, to have been the Florentine goldsmith, Baccio Baldini, but there is no reliable ground for this attribution, and the true author is unknown. The technique is that of an unpractised hand, and has nothing to distinguish it from the average work of contemporary Florentine engravers. In spite, however, of their slight artistic merit, the plates have a special interest in their connection with Botticelli.

Botticelli's drawings for eight of the first nineteen cantos of the Inferno are missing, whereas for the remaining eleven we have not only his drawings, but the prints of the Florentine edition of 1481. A com-

Illustration to Canto XXXI of the Inferno. From a Dante Manuscript of the XIV century in the British Museum

parison of the prints with the drawings shews that the engraver was intimately acquainted with Botticelli's compositions, and must have made use of them for his own work. He did not, actually copy them, but he borrowed the chief features of the arrangement and grouping. These he crowded together in the narrow space at his command, occasionally adding some feeble invention of his own, and so piecing out his illustrations more or less successfully. In judging of these and kindred prints we must bear in mind that their primary aim was utilitarian rather than æsthetic or artistic; they were intended mainly to point out the contents of each canto, and impress it upon the reader's memory, a purpose they actually fulfilled far better than a verbal table of contents, and this explains why so many fine editions of Dante published in the fifteenth and sixteenth centuries are furnished with these small, and from the artistic point of view, insignificant vignettes. On closer examination of such a series as that in the Venetian edition of 1491, we see what an excellent guide they are to the reader. We give a reproduction of one of these vignettes. The letters D. and V. above the figures signify Dante and Virgil.

The prints in the Florentine edition, however, have a double interest for us. In the first place, we may gather from them some general idea of the nine missing Botticelli drawings (Inferno II to VII, IX, XI, and XIV). The date of publication of the volume further makes it evident that Botticelli must have begun to work on the Dante before 1481. His journey to Rome in the summer of 1481, and the execution of the Vatican frescoes, no doubt caused him to lay aside the drawings for a time. Very probably he had only completed the illustration of the first nineteen cantos when he left Florence. The engraver was therefore unable to proceed with his work; but the printer, having already completed the text, brought out the volume in August 1481, while Botticelli was in Rome, without waiting for the rest of the drawings. The edition therefore appeared in the incomplete state with which we are familiar.

After his return to Florence, Botticelli again set to work upon the Dante designs. The time he spent on them and perhaps also his absorption in the text, may have caused a certain neglect of more remunerative work. This, and perhaps also differences with the printer or editor he had disappointed, may have given rise to those complications in his affairs alluded to by Vasari. The latter was not alone in his ignorance of the Dante drawings executed for Lorenzo di Pierfrancesco; it seems to have been shared by the artist's contemporaries generally. Strange to say, the work remained entirely unnoticed until our own day. The woodcuts in the edition of Dante, published at Brescia in 1487 and those in two others which appeared at Venice in 1491, shew, indeed, a certain affinity with Botticelli's drawings, being obviously free copies of the plates in the Florentine edition of 1481. The process by which this adaptation was accomplished may be readily traced, if we compare the vignette, from the Venetian volume, reproduced above, with our further reproduction of the plate illustrating the canto of the Inferno in the Florentine edition. From the nineteenth canto, where the Florentine plates come to an end, all resemblance to Botticelli's drawings disappears from the woodcuts, a proof that the draughtsman of the latter had access to the engravings, but not to the original drawings.

We must pass on to the sixteenth century, to find an artist who was undoubtedly inspired by Botticelli's actual handiwork, and not by the Florentine engravings. The Roman painter, Federigo Zucchero, illustrated the Divine Comedy in a series of large drawings, carried out partly with the pen, partly in red and black chalk. Eighty-eight of these are now in the Uffizi collection. Zucchero's autograph inscriptions on the sheets shew them to have been executed at the Escurial about 1586-1587, during his first visit to Spain.

In several of these there is such a close resemblance, both in the backgrounds and the arrangement of the figures, to the corresponding designs by Botticelli, that the connection can hardly be a merely fortuitous one. Zucchero either made his drawings under the immediate influence of Botticelli's originals, or was inspired by studies from them. His indebtedness to Botticelli is obvious, for instance, in the illustrations of Purgatorio XIII and XIV, notably in the figure of the old man, and various other details. Even in the treatment, he occasionally caught something of Botticelli's handling, especially in the delineation of the gigantic Satan, where he has closely followed the Botticellian conception. Where Zucchero became acquainted with Botticelli's work, whether in Spain or Italy, remains as obscure a question as the general history of our Codex.

Vignette to Canto VIII of the Inferno.
From a Venetian edition of Dante published in [illegible]

The far-reaching influence of Dante throughout the period of the Renaissance manifests itself under the most varied forms, both in art and literature. The oft repeated attempt to give visible form to his creations illustrates but a single phase of his power over the minds of men. Many of the draughtsmen who were fascinated by the theme were unequal to the task they undertook, as was the case with Zucchero. The only work of the kind which would have formed a worthy pendant to that of Botticelli is lost to us for ever. Michelangelo is known to have illustrated the entire poem with pen drawings made on the wide margins of a printed edition. The precious volume became the property of one Antonio Montauti, a Florentine sculptor (died 1740), who, removing to Rome for the execution of certain works, sent his household goods thither by sea, Michelangelo's Dante among them. The ship containing the priceless treasure was wrecked off Civitavecchia. A happier fate has guarded Botticelli's work for us throughout the changes of four centuries.

INFERNO

THE DIAGRAM OF THE INFERNO. This drawing, which is elaborately coloured in the original, forms a kind of an introductory and explanatory chart for the Inferno illustrations. It covers the front page of the sheet of parchment, on the reverse of which is the drawing for Canto I.

According to Dante's conception, Hell is a funnel-shaped structure, extending from the upper surface of the earth to its central point. The funnel or cone is enclosed at the top by a vault, on which stands the city of Jerusalem, and consists of a vestibule, and nine circles, the successive circles of course narrowing as they approach the lower end of the cone. Each of the last three circles is divided into several subcircles; making in all twenty-four compartments. Sinners expiate their offences in different circles, according to their degrees of guilt: the greater the criminal, the lower the place of his imprisonment. The illustration gives a vertical section of the cone, and the various circles have the appearance of superposed horizontal strata. In these are numerous groups of small figures, arranged for the most part as in the illustrations to the Inferno. The execution of detail is careful, but the artist was evidently more concerned to give a comprehensible plan of the infernal regions, than to express an artistic conception. The last circle becomes so small, owing to the narrowing of the cone, that a distinct portrayal of its scenes was impossible, and it is therefore reproduced on a larger scale at the bottom of the sheet in a sort of supplementary design.

The rocks of which the structure is composed are painted in brown and yellow tones, against which the little figures are relieved in light and varied tints. The drawing is enclosed in a border of pale gold-leaf. The colours may never have taken kindly to the uneven surface of the parchment. They have scaled off in many places, and the whole surface has been further injured by rubbing.

4*

I

Dante has lost his way in a gloomy forest. Emerging from the thicket, he finds himself at the foot of a hill, the summit of which is touched by the rays of the rising sun. He attempts to ascend, but is driven back, first by a spotted panther, then by a lion and a she-wolf. He turns to re-enter the forest, but the poet Virgil appears, and offers to be his guide.

*ENGRAVING OF 1481.** The composition of the plate agrees with that of the drawing in arrangement, and in many of the details: the positions of Dante and Virgil are almost identical in the two, saving that Dante's figure appears five times in the drawing, and only three times in the print.

II

ENGRAVING OF 1481. Dante shews signs of wavering in his resolve to follow Virgil. Virgil encourages him, and declares himself sent by Beatrice to be his guide. The two poets stand on a "dark coast" (V. 40). The entrance to Hell, with the first words of the inscription over the portal "Per me" are shewn in the print, though these are first

* We give this title to the plates in the Florentine Edition of Dante, published in 1481. (See p. 20.) The reproductions given here are slightly reduced facsimiles of the originals.

introduced in the following canto of the poem. Above, in a glory, is a female figure, to which Virgil points, while Dante gazes upward. The

figure doubtless represents Beatrice, and is an addition of the artist's, for Beatrice is only mentioned in the poem, and does not appear.

III

ENGRAVING OF 1481. Dante and Virgil at the Gate of Hell. The first words of the three opening lines of the inscription: "Per me . . ." are legible above the entrance.

The two poets enter the Vestibule of the "Neutrals", the dark abode of naked, wailing spirits, who lived on earth "without or praise or blame". The long procession follows a banner, borne by a devil, of whom there is no mention in the text.

The poets come to the banks of Acheron. Charon approaches in a boat to convey the souls of the damned across the river. The poem describes him as an old man; in the print he is represented as a devil. Virgil converses with Charon. A deafening storm arises, by which Dante is stunned. He falls to the ground, as if overtaken by sudden sleep. His prostrate form appears in the extreme corner of the print to the right.

THE SECOND ENGRAVING TO THE THIRD CANTO OF THE INFERNO is a reversed replica of all the main features of the first print, much weaker, however, in every respect. The incident of the souls of the damned swimming in the Styx, and trying to lay hold of Charon's boat, is an interpolation, for which there is no authority in the text.

This print appears in a few copies of the Florentine edition of the Commedia published in 1481, and is generally placed at the foot of the opening page of the first chapter, the original forming the head-piece above. The drawing and general treatment of the replica shew it to have been executed by a hand inferior to that which produced the remaining illustrations.

IV

ENGRAVING OF 1481. This illustration, condensed and pregnant to a fault, touches very slightly on the main incidents of the canto, so far as its earlier verses are concerned.

Roused from his swoon by a clap of thunder, Dante finds himself on the edge of a precipice, descending which with Virgil, he enters the first circle of Hell. They leave behind them a great multitude, the souls of those who lived blamelessly, but died unbaptized, and advance towards a flame, by the light of which they discern four mighty shades, Homer, armed with a sword, Horace, Ovid, and Lucan. In company with these they pass on to the beacon-light, and come to a fortress, encircled by seven walls, and a pleasant stream. They enter, through seven successive gates. On a green lawn in the centre of the fortress they discover the shades of many illustrious men and women of antiquity. Aristotle sits enthroned among his scholars. (Dante and Virgil quit the fortress.)

V

ENGRAVING OF 1481. In the second circle of Hell, Dante and Virgil behold Minos, judging the souls of the departed. As they confess their sins, Minos indicates the number of the circle to which they are condemned by coiling his tail round his body a corresponding number of times, then hurls them downward to their appointed places. Minos addresses a warning to Dante, and is informed by Virgil of his special mission. As they advance, they hear the roaring of a tempest, and see the souls of carnal sinners, driven onward by a furious wind. Dante

notices a couple who float through the air pressing closely one against the other. (Francesca da Rimini and Paolo Malatesta. He addresses them. Francesca relates her story.)

VI

ENGRAVING OF 1481. Dante and Virgil in the third circle. Heavy showers of rain, snow, and hail fall on the souls of the gluttonous, who do penance here; they lie naked on the ground, the three-headed dog, Cerberus, tearing their flesh, and rending them limb from limb. Virgil quiets the monster by throwing handfuls of earth into his maw, as he gapes at the advancing travellers. The poets pass over the prostrate shades. Dante converses with the Florentine Ciacco. (Dante and Virgil continue their descent.)

VII

ENGRAVING OF 1481. The two poets encounter Pluto. Virgil speaks to him of the Archangel Michael, upon which the fiendish monster falls to the ground,

> "As sails, full spread and bellying with the wind
> Drop suddenly collapsed, if the mast split." (V. 13-14.)

Dante and Virgil enter the fourth circle, where the prodigal and the avaricious are condemned to roll great weights against each other, breast to breast. They rush forward in two opposing ranks, and after the encounter, turn round, and begin their onslaught afresh. Among them are many ecclesiastics, distinguishable by their tonsured heads.

The second part of the canto, which sets forth the sufferings of the wrathful and morose in a loathsome slough, is unnoticed in this illustration, but is represented in that of the following canto.

VIII

Passing along the banks of the muddy pool in which the wrathful are immersed, the poets come to a tower. (Cf. the close of the preceding canto.) As they approach, two signal-lights flame out from its summit, which are answered by a corresponding flame in the distance. Diverging slightly from the text, Botticelli has made the answering beacon also a double flame. Phlegyas hastily approaches in his skiff, and at the command of Virgil, rows the two poets over the Stygian marsh. The Florentine Filippo Argenti, emerging from the waters, catches at the boat with both hands. Dante and Virgil repulse him. Fetching a wide circuit, they come at last to the walls and gates of the fiery city of Dis. A host of demons rush out to meet them, and prevent their entrance, more especially that of the still living Dante. Virgil parleys with them in vain. He comforts his despairing companion by promises of speedy help.

In the illustration, Botticelli recurs to the preceding canto on the one hand, and on the other, inserts various details from that which follows. In the background to the right, Dante and Virgil are seen ascending from the fourth abyss; to the left, they arrive at the base of the tower in Phlegyas' boat. The souls of the wrathful appear in the waters of the lake. The arrival at the gates of Dis, and Virgil's parley with the devils, is depicted to the left. Within the walls of the city are shewn the fiery graves of the heretics, described in the ninth canto.

ENGRAVING OF 1481. The print agrees with the drawing as regards the episodes of the passage across the Styx, the meeting with Argenti, and the arrival of the poets at the walls of the flaming city.

IX

As Dante and Virgil converse at the fiery gateway of Dis, the three Furies, Megæra, Alecto, and Tisiphone appear above the portal girdled with serpents, their heads crowned with asps and adders in place of hair. They scream at the wanderers, and invoke the aid of the Gorgon, to save Dante from the sight of which, Virgil exhorts him to close his eyes, and even covers them with his own hands. A devil, standing behind the Furies on the tower, holds up the head of the Gorgon. Borne on a whirlwind, a heavenly messenger passes dryfooted across the Styx, the souls of the damned fleeing before him. He reaches the gate of the city, and touches it with his wand, whereupon it flies open, and Dante and Virgil enter. They find themselves in an open space, full of flaming sepulchres, the lid of each suspended above it. From within the tombs the poets hear the groans and cries of tortured heretics and their followers.

ENGRAVING OF 1481. The plate differs a good deal from the drawing. The Gorgon, which appears behind the Furies on the tower in the latter, is here represented borne forward by a devil to the right. Many details of the composition are altered; the flaming graves of the drawing are omitted in the print.

X

The poets proceed along a narrow pathway between the ramparts and the fiery graves. The lids of the tombs are raised. (Virgil discourses of the souls within.) Dante hears a voice calling to him, that of the Ghibelline Farinato degli Uberti, who raises himself from the waist upwards out of his grave. Another shade, that of Cavalcante dei Cavalcanti, rises beside him, resting his chin on the edge of the tomb, and also addresses Dante.

The poets continue their path to the left. To avoid the horrible exhalations from the abyss in the centre of the plain (Inf. XI, 4-12), they take refuge for a time under the lid of a great sepulchre, on which is inscribed: "I guard Pope Anastasius". (Anastasius, Pope A. D. 496, is placed by Dante among the heretics, on account of his leanings towards the Arian schism.)

ENGRAVING OF 1481. The print repeats nearly all the motives of the drawing, from which, however, it differs considerably in arrangement. The composition is reversed.

XI

ENGRAVING OF 1481. Descending to the seventh circle, Dante and Virgil come to a rocky bank of ruins. They take refuge behind the lid of a huge tomb, to escape the noisome exhalations from below. On the tomb is inscribed "I guard Pope Anastasius". (Cf. the illustration to

the tenth canto). (Here they gradually become accustomed to the foul air, and after a while are able to endure it. Virgil discourses to Dante of the various circles and their inhabitants.)

The flaming graves of the arch-heretics are still to be seen in the upper part of the print. (Cf. Inf. X.)

XII

Descending a rocky passage in the precipice, they come to the seventh circle. The Minotaur lies extended on the verge of the abyss, and, enraged at the sight of the travellers, furiously gnaws his own body. Virgil orders him hence, and he plunges aside, "like a bull under its death-stroke". They step downward from crag to crag of the rock, supposed to have been riven at the birth of Christ, and reach a deep ditch shaped like a bow, extending across the wide plain. The ditch is filled with seething blood, in which lie the souls of the damned who injured their fellow-men by violence and rapine. They are more or less deeply immersed in proportion to the extent of their guilt. The flood rises to the eyebrows of tyrants. Centaurs on the banks shoot arrows at all who emerge from the blood further than is consistent with their guilt. Three of the Centaurs, Nessus, Chiron, and Pholus, detach themselves from the herd, and advance with threatening mien to meet the travellers. Virgil subdues them. He persuades Chiron to send one of his companions with them as guide. Nessus conducts them along the

shores of the stream to a spot where the blood becomes so shallow that it only covers the feet. Here they cross the channel, and Nessus returns. (On the way, Nessus points out to them some famous sinners, expiating their crimes in the bloody tide.)

ENGRAVING OF 1481. The print follows the drawing very closely, reproducing the main motives, but reversing the composition.

XIII

Dante and Virgil pass on to the second division of the seventh circle. They find themselves in a dense thicket of gnarled and thorny trees, in which the Harpies build their nests. Dante hears on all sides cries and lamentations, but cannot discern whence they come. The thorn-bushes are, in fact, the transformed shades of suicides. Incited by Virgil, Dante breaks off a branch, whereupon blood flows down the trunk, and the tree breaks forth into a complaint of the suffering inflicted on it by the poet. The speaker is Piero delle Vigne, Chancellor to the Emperor Frederick II., who, falling into disgrace with his master, killed himself in prison. Further on, Dante sees two shades pursued by black mastiffs. These are the prodigals, Lano of Siena, and Jacopo da Sant' Andrea of

Padua. Jacopo takes refuge in one of the bushes, but is torn to pieces by the dogs together with the bush. The lacerated trunk—a Florentine—intreats Dante to gather his scattered branches, and lay them at his roots.

ENGRAVING OF 1481. The print is a condensed version of the chief motives of the drawing, given in reverse.

XIV

ENGRAVING OF 1481. The third round of the seventh circle. Dante and Virgil, emerging from the thicket, come to an arid, sandy plain, where blasphemers, Sodomites, and usurers do penance. Flames fall upon them like snow-flakes; they endeavour to shield themselves from the fiery shower with their uplifted hands. Some lie prone on the ground, others sit in a crouching posture, but the greater number run distractedly to and fro. One, who lies apparently indifferent to the falling

flames, Virgil explains to be Capaneus (V. 61). The red stream of Phlegethon rises in the thicket. (Cf. Inf. XIII.)

XV

Passing along the shores of Phlegethon, which is compassed by rocky dams, Dante and Virgil encounter a troop of the naked souls tormented in the sandy waste (cf. Inf. XVI, 35). (They are the Sodomites.) One of the shades addresses Dante, who recognizes his former tutor, Brunetto Latini. Dante stretches his hand downwards to Latini, who begs him to continue his way, conversing with him as he walks. (Their discourse forms the rest of the canto.)

The drawing is painted in body-colour, and, unlike the other illustrations, is arranged somewhat like a plan, so that the spectator seems to be gazing downwards from a high point of sight on the plain below, with its moving figures.

ENGRAVING OF 1481. The print, while introducing fewer figures, gives a selection from the leading motives of the drawing. In both, the stream flows to the left, and lies to the right of the wide plain, on which are scattered the figures of the damned. But whereas Dante,

Virgil, and Latini, are on the right bank of the river in the drawing, in the print they appear on the left.

XVI

Continuing their way along the banks of Phlegethon, Dante and Virgil encounter another band of Sodomites, doing penance in the sea of sand and shower of flames. The poets come to a place where the river forms a cascade, leaping over the rocky wall that divides the seventh from the eighth circle. Three shades, hovering round Dante, engage him in speech. They are the Florentines, Guidoguerra, Tegghiaio Aldobrandi, and Jacopo Rusticucci.

At the edge of the abyss into which thunder the dark waters of Phlegethon, Dante, at Virgil's command, unfastens a rope from his waist, and lets it down into the gulf. The many-coloured monster, Geryon, ascends forthwith and supports himself at the edge of the rampart.

In the drawing, Botticelli shews Geryon's head and fore-paws, appearing in the left-hand lower corner. The usurers, of whom a further account is given in the following canto, are seated in a group at the edge of the precipice, under a shower of flame. Each has a pouch slung round his neck.

ENGRAVING OF 1481. The composition of the plate differs considerably from that of the drawing. The group of Dante and the three Florentines is brought forward, and to the left are two of the usurers.

XVII

Dante and Virgil on the edge of the precipice that descends to the eighth circle. The monster Geryon reclines on the dam. (Cf. the close of the last canto.) He has the face of a just man, and the body of a serpent. His back, breast, and sides are gaily patterned.

> . . . . Colours variegated more
> Nor Turks nor Tartars e'er on cloth of state
> With interchangeable embroidery wove (V. 15-17).

His tail ends in a fork, charged with poison, like that of the scorpion. He lies with his breast on the upper ledge of the dyke, and beats the air with his tail. The two poets are in the act of descending from the river bank to approach Geryon on the edge of the cataract.

Dante turns aside to speak to the shades who sit on the confines of the sandy desert, endeavouring to ward off the falling flames with their hands. They are usurers. Each has a pouch slung round his neck with his blazon or sign, upon it. Dante describes several of the armorial bearings and emblems. These are not given, however, in the drawing.

Virgil mounts on Geryon's back, and exhorts Dante to follow his example. With much fear and hesitation he obeys, seating himself in front of Virgil, who clasps him in his arms. Geryon carries them downward through the air. (Alighting with them at the bottom of the abyss, he leaves them hastily, and disappears.)

ENGRAVING OF 1481. The leading motive of the drawing is based on the description of Virgil, seated on Geryon's back, encouraging Dante, who still hesitates, to mount in front of him. The engraver distinguishes two of the usurers by the emblazoned pouches described in the poem. He who bears the lion is Gianfigliazzi (V. 59-60), the other, with the goose, Ubbriacchi of Florence. The composition of the drawing is not reversed in this print.

XVIII

In the upper left hand corner of the drawing, Dante and Virgil are represented standing at the base of the precipice, while Geryon hastens from them to the right. The bottom of the gulf in which they find themselves consists of a circular space, divided into ten trenches, each like the moat surrounding a fortress or castle. These moats, the Malebolge, are divided one from another by dykes, spanned by rock-hewn bridges which connect the dams. In the centre of the space is a deep spring. The eighteenth canto treats of the first and second Bolgia, both of which Botticelli depicts.

In the first Bolgia the shades of seducers run along in double rows, each row facing the opposite way from the other. Devils with leathern thongs lash them from the dykes above (V. 25). One of the shades hangs down his head, to escape the scrutiny of Dante, who nevertheless recognizes in him Venedico Caccianimico of Bologna. (They converse together.)

Passing on the bridge that spans the second Bolgia, Dante beholds the penance of flatterers, immersed in filth from head to foot. He recognizes Alessio Interminei (Interminelli) of Lucca: Virgil points out to him Thaïs, crouching in the filth, and tearing her hair.

This drawing is painted in body-colour, but there are evidences that the colouring was not completed by the master in accordance with his first intention.

ENGRAVING OF 1481. This gives but a very inadequate idea of the general composition of the drawing. Geryon is relegated to the middle-distance in the upper part of the plate. So far as a comparison of print and drawing is permissible, in such details, for instance, as the position of the bridges, and the attitudes of Dante and Virgil in relation to the figures in the moats, the print retains the arrangement of the drawing, without reversing it.

XIX

Dante and Virgil pass on to the third Bolgia, in which are the souls of those convicted of simony, or traffic in spiritual things. These are fixed head downwards, in round holes in the ground, so that no more of them than the legs appears without. Flames play upon the souls of their feet. One among them, who writhes as if in greater agony than his companions, attracts Dante's notice. Virgil carries the poet down the incline into the chasm, where he interrogates the tortured sinner, Pope Nicholas V.

Virgil then catches Dante in his arms, and ascends with him to the summit of the bridge connecting the fourth and fifth causeways. In the background of the drawing, the Bolgia of the flatterers, described in the last canto, is again introduced.

ENGRAVING OF 1481. The print adheres, on the whole, pretty closely to the drawing, omitting, however, some of the figures. The composition is not reversed. The two groups, Dante and Virgil descending to the simoniacs, and Virgil carrying Dante back, are to the right of the bridge in the print, and to the left in the drawing.

XX

The fourth chasm of the eighth circle, the abode of soothsayers, and wizards. Their punishment is to have their faces reversed, the heads being violently twisted round on the bodies, because, while on earth, they desired to look too far forward. They pace mournfully along, weeping in silence. Only two of the band are sufficiently prominent in the drawing to enable us to identify them from Dante's descriptions, the bearded Eurypylus above, to the right (V. 106-112), and Manto, the sorceress spoken of in V. 52 *et seq.*

XXI

The fifth gulf of the eighth circle, where public peculators are imprisoned in a stream of burning pitch. Devils thrust them back into the pitch with hooks whenever they rise above the surface. Dante and Virgil stand on the rocky bridge that spans the stream. The latter gazes with horror at a devil, who has just brought in one of the chief magistrates of Lucca (Martino Bottaio, according to Ottimo's commentary) and cast him into the lake of pitch. Below, in the centre of the drawing, Dante is shewn endeavouring to hide among the rocks (V. 58-60). Virgil subdues the demons, who rush out furiously against him, by an account of his mission and authority. He then summons Dante from his hiding-place, and the poets continue their way, escorted by eleven devils. In order to reach the sixth Bolgia, they are obliged to make a *détour* into the fifth.

XXII

Dante and Virgil skirt the shores of the lake of pitch in the fifth gulf. Those who are tormented in the boiling flood occasionally rise for an instant to the surface, disappearing again beneath. One, who ventures to emerge too far, is drawn to land by one of the devils, and suffers further tortures. At Dante's request, Virgil questions him. He replies that he was an unfaithful servant of the King of Navarre, Thibault II. Barbariccia, the leader of the eleven devils who accompany Dante and Virgil, holds him fast with his hook, while Virgil converses with him.

Two of the devils fall into the lake, and are fished out by their companions (V. 140 *et seq.*).

At the top of the sheet the figures of the soothsayers and magicians of the fourth chasm are seen pacing along a rocky ledge, as described in the twentieth canto.

XXIII

To the left, in the upper corner of the drawing, Dante and Virgil, who have just left the fifth gulf, pace slowly forward, one behind the other, like "minor friars, journeying on their road". Dante fears lest the demons, incensed against Virgil and himself, should presently pursue them. His fears being shortly realized, Virgil seizes him in his arms, and slides down the precipitous descent into the sixth chasm. Here the demons of the fifth gulf have no power. Dante and Virgil find in the depths of the sixth Bolgia the scene depicted in the lower part of the drawing. Hypocrites march slowly and painfully along, shrouded in cowls, overlaid with gold on the outside, but formed of lead within. Dante is shewn conversing with Catalano and Loderingo of Bologna. Lying on the ground, naked and crucified, are Caiaphas, Annas, and various members of the Council of the Pharisees. (S. John XI, 47.) The sinners in the leaden cowls pass over their prostrate bodies.

XXIV

Climbing with difficulty over the ruins of the shattered bridge, Dante and Virgil reach the seventh gulf, where thieves and robbers undergo their punishment. Their hands are bound together behind them with serpents; and in front, serpents bore through their brains and loins.

In the centre of the foreground, Vanni Fucci, the pillager of a church at Pistoja, is attacked by a fiery serpent, the bite of which causes him to crumble into ashes; the ashes, however, immediately resume their human form. Below, to the right, Vanni Fucci is shewn conversing with Dante, and foretelling the future defeat of the Bianchi. The artist again shews the spectator a portion of the last gulf, and a few of the figures in the leaden cowls are seen to the left, coming forward from behind a wall of rock.

XXV

The canto opens with the blasphemies of the sacriligious Vanni Fucci. Serpents seize him again, and he rushes away without further speech. To the right, Botticelli shews the Centaur, Cacus, advancing towards Fucci.

To the left of the drawing, a six-footed serpent seizes Agnello Brunelleschi, with whom it becomes incorporated. (V. 50 *et seq.*) The transformations of men into serpents, and of serpents into men are typified by a variety of monstrous forms. Dante and Virgil appear twice in the foreground, half their bodies only rising over the edge of the abyss. In the upper part of the drawing we again see the hypocrites in their leaden habits. (Inf. XXIII.)

XXVI

Re-ascending the face of the cliff, Dante and Virgil reach the eighth gulf of Malebolge, where evil counsellors are enveloped in flames. A flame, divided into two tongues, enshrouds Ulysses and Diomedes. Their faces are visible through the fire. As the forked flame approaches the poets, Virgil, at Dante's request, addresses Ulysses, who describes the last of his voyages.

XXVII

Dante and Virgil still in the eighth gulf of the eighth circle. They converse with another of the flame-shrouded shades, Guido da Montefeltro.

XXVIII

The ninth gulf of the eighth circle, which contains the promoters of divisions and discords. They move about with maimed limbs, and divided bodies. As soon as the fissures re-unite, devils cleave them asunder once more. Such is notably the punishment of Mahomet, the author of the greatest religious schism ever known, who is, no doubt represented by the figure in the upper part of the drawing, somewhat to the left of the centre. The figure close to Mahomet, advancing towards the left, is Mahomet's son-in-law, Ali, the promoter of a further schism in Mahommedanism itself. Others, mentioned in the poem as undergoing a like penance, are characterized by Botticelli, among them Piero da Medicina, and Mosca Lamberti. The figure holding out his own head to Dante, is the troubadour, Bertrand de Born, who incited Prince Henry of England (the "Young King") to rebel against his father, Henry II.

XXIX

In the upper part of the drawing Dante and Virgil are standing upon the bridge of the ninth chasm, Bertrand de Born holding up his head to them from below. A rock-hewn dyke divides this gulf from the tenth, in which coiners and alchemists do penance, tormented by various diseases. They scrape the scurf from their bodies with their nails. In the foreground to the right, Dante and Virgil pause to converse with two of the damned, seated back to back on the ground. One is an alchemist, Griffolino of Arezzo, the other a Florentine coiner, Capocchio.

A group to the right of the drawing refers to an episode in the following canto, V. 25 *et seq.* The man, running forward, and the woman who fastens her teeth into his flesh from behind, can only be intended for Giovanni Schicchi (Inf. XXX, 31) and Myrrha (ib. V. 38).

XXX

The illustration to this canto is a mere sketch. The poets still linger in the tenth gulf. To the right, Botticelli indicates the bridge on which they stand by a few curving lines. Beyond is the figure of the coiner, Adam of Brescia, his body swollen with dropsy (V. 49 et seq.), and three other figures, very lightly sketched.

XXXI

As he approaches the rampart of the last gulf, Dante hears the blast of a horn. Ranged along the wall, he sees gigantic forms, which at first he takes for towers. They are, however, fettered giants, who, standing in the well-like cavity of the ninth circle, tower aloft into the eighth. The blower of the horn is Nimrod, and the fettered figure, whose back is turned to the spectator, is Ephialtes. At Virgil's request, Antæus lifts the two poets, and places them at the bottom of the last circle.

XXXII

Dante and Virgil have reached the first division of the last circle, the Caïna, so-named after the first fratricide. They stand on the frozen lake, in the ice of which are imprisoned the murderers of their kinsfolk. Dante converses with Alessandro and Napoleone degli Alberti, whose bodies are frozen together. On the rampart above, the feet of the giants are visible (cf. Inf. XXXI, V. 31 et seq.).

Adjoining the Caïna is the "Antenora", the division set apart for the betrayers of their fatherland (from Antenor, the Trojan, who suggested to the Greeks the stratagem of the wooden horse). Dante seizes one of the frozen inmates by the hair, and compels him to reveal his name. It is Bocca degli Abbati. Passing on, the poets come to Count Ugolino della Gherardesca, who is gnawing the skull of the Archbishop Ruggieri degli Ubaldini. Part of this drawing refers to the next canto. Above the circle of the Caïna is written the word "Chaina", above the next division "antenora".

XXXIII

This drawing shews the four divisions of the lake of ice, the Caïna, the Antenora, the Ptolemea (from Ptolemy, see Maccab. XVI, 11-16), and Giudecca (from Judas Iscariot). Dante and Virgil are shewn conversing with Ugolino in the Antenora, and below, in the Ptolemea, with Alberigo de' Manfredi of Faenza, whose body remains on earth, apparently alive, though his soul is already in hell. The damned lie prone on their backs, the tears freezing in their eyes (V. 93-99). The division in the foreground, the Giudecca, is left blank.

XXXIV

Botticelli devotes two drawings to the thirty-fourth canto. The first represents the upper half of Lucifer, three-headed, and with bat-like wings, as described in V. 38-50. In the mouth of the central head he champs the body of Judas Iscariot, tearing with his claws the part of his prey that hangs outside his jaws. The traitors Brutus and Cassius are in the other mouths.

The second drawing shews the whole figure of Satan, on a page twice the size of the other illustrations, and formed of two sheets of vellum fastened together. At various intervals, the figures of Dante and Virgil are shewn, climbing along the monster, and clinging to the frozen locks of his shaggy fell. At the central point of the universe, they turn, and still climbing upwards towards the feet of Satan, enter a cavernous path, whence they emerge into the open air.

PURGATORIO

I

In the illustration to this canto Botticelli recurs to the closing lines of the Inferno, shewing, in the centre of the drawing, the figures of Dante and Virgil emerging from the cleft in the rocks, through which, after following the course of a brook, they gain the open air (Inf. XXXIV, 133 *et seq.*). They perceive an old man of dignified appearance on the plain before them. It is Cato of Utica. (They converse with him.) The figures of Dante and Virgil, and the episode of Dante bowing reverently before Cato at Virgil's command, are very lightly sketched in outline. Virgil is shewn washing Dante's face by the waterside, and girding him with rushes, as directed by Cato.

To the left of the drawing we note various episodes related in the following canto. In the background, touched in very lightly with the point, is the ship, in which departed souls are conveyed to Purgatory. An angel propels the boat with his wings (Purg. II, 26-33). Some of the souls are depicted hastening up the bank (ib. 50).

In the background is the mountain of Purgatory, with its various divisions.

Below, on the edge of the drawing are the opening words of the first canto:

1 perchore miglior aqua
(Per correr migliori acque).

II

Here a scene already depicted in the foregoing illustration is again introduced, but in greater detail.

The souls conveyed to the shores of Purgatory disembark when the Angel makes the sign of the cross (V. 49-50). The Angel then departs with the boat.

The souls enquire of Dante and Virgil the way to the mountain, and are much astonished to find a living person—Dante—in their midst.

Dante recognizes the singer, Casella, and fain would embrace him, but finds his shade impalpable to his clasp. Cato admonishes the souls to proceed, and they hastily resume their course. The departing figures are very slightly sketched. At the bottom of the drawing the opening line of the second canto is written as follows:

2 gia era il sole al orezonte
(Già era il sole all' orizzonte).

III

Dante and Virgil proceed from the shore of Purgatory towards the mountain. (The sun being behind them, Dante's body projects a shadow, whereas the rays pass through the immaterial form of Virgil.) Dante, alarmed at this phenomenon, is reassured by Virgil.

They reach the base of the mountain, which they find so steep, that they despair of climbing it. "On the left hand" (Dante's left hand, therefore to the right in the picture) they perceive a troop of spirits standing closely together on the crags. Virgil enquires of them where he may find some declivity in the mountain-wall. Amazed at Dante's corporeal presence, they stand with downcast eyes and timid mien, while Virgil explains the presence of a mortal among them. (Dante converses with Manfred, King of Naples.)

Supplementing the images of the poet, as if to emphasize the scene of action, and its connection with the preceding canto, Botticelli has introduced a group of souls arriving on the shores of Purgatory, and, in the distance, the angel returning across the waters with his boat (Purg. II). The opening line of Canto III is inscribed on the edge of the drawing:

3 avegnia che la subitana fugha
(Avvegna che la subitana fuga).

IV

The poets pass along the steep base of the mountain with the spirits, who agree to shew them where to ascend. They come to a narrow cleft in the rocks, whereupon the spirits exclaim in chorus that here is the path they desire. Dante and Virgil press forward laboriously in the narrow path. Weary with climbing, Dante is encouraged by Virgil to persevere, and they reach a projecting cornice, on which they seat themselves to rest. They face towards the East, and discuss the position of the sun, which Dante now perceives to be on his left. Resting under the shade of a neighbouring rock, they note a group of spirits, among whom Dante recognizes the Florentine Belacqua, an accomplished musician. (He converses with Belacqua.) The opening words of the canto at the bottom of the page are partly effaced:

4 quando per dilectan . .
(Quando per dilettanze).

V

As Dante and Virgil leave the resting spirits, one among them remarks that Dante's gestures are those of a living person, and that his body throws a shadow. Virgil commands him to pay no heed to the whispers of the spirits (V. 1-15). The group introduced by Botticelli in the lower part of the drawing refers to this incident. Approaching them along the side of the hill, the poets perceive a group of spirits, who advance, singing the *Miserere.* When they note the substantiality of Dante's body, they cease their song, and two of their number, running forward, enquire as to the condition of the wanderers. Virgil informs them that Dante is a living person, and bids them tell their comrades. The spirits then cluster round Dante. They are the souls of such as died by violence, but who, nevertheless, were granted time for repentance in their last hours. They beseech Dante to obtain for them the prayers of their friends, when he shall have returned to the world. (Three of the spirits are introduced by name in the poem, and give an account of themselves.) Under the drawing are the opening words of the fifth canto:

5 i era gia da quel ombre parttito
(Io era già da quell' ombre partito).

VI

Dante disengages himself with some difficulty from the shades who cluster round him. Continuing his journey, he enquires of Virgil whether the prayers of mortals ever avail to influence the decrees of Heaven. Virgil refers him to Beatrice, whom he shall meet at the summit of the mountain.

They encounter a solitary spirit, who gazes fixedly at them. As Virgil approaches him to enquire the way, the shade—who is Sordello, the Mantuan Troubadour—joyfully greets the poet as his compatriot. The group formed by Sordello and Virgil, with a number of spirits gathered round them, is very faintly sketched with the silver point in the upper part of the drawing. Below are the opening words of the canto:

6 quando siparte el giuocho dela zara
(Quando si parte il giuoco della zara).

VII

Sordello inclines himself reverently before Virgil (V. 15), and clasps him round the knees. The sun is setting, and the wanderers are anxious to continue their journey. Sordello warns them that after nightfall, they are powerless to ascend the mountain. He draws a line with his finger on the earth, saying:—

". . . . this line
Thou shalt not over pass, soon as the sun
Hath disappeared." (V. 53-54.)

Sordello conducts them by a crooked path "betwixt the steep and plain" to a recess in the mountain side, gay with flowers, where abide the souls of many kings and princes, who, absorbed in cares of state, deferred their own repentance and atonement over long.

Only that part of the composition which refers to the first division of the canto, and treats of the meeting with Sordello, is executed with the pen. The portions of the drawing to the right, and to the lower part of the page are merely sketched in silver point, with the exception of one or two figures, such as that seated to the left, wearing the papal tiara, and the bearded man addressing him. Both of these are more elaborately treated. At the bottom of the page is the first verse of the Canto:—

7 poscia che lachoglenze oneste e liete
(Poscia che l' accoglienze oneste e liete).

VIII

This design, which the artist evidently intended to treat with great elaboration and richness of detail, was never carried beyond the first light sketch with the silver-point. The principal groups are barely distinguishable.

Sordello has brought Dante and Virgil to the valley, in which the souls of the princes whose tardy repentance is spoken of in Canto VII, do penance. Dante perceives two angels armed with blunt swords, descending from the heights above, their draperies floating behind them. One of the angels alights near Dante, the other on the opposite boundary of the vale. Sordello informs the poets that the angels have come to defend the valley from a serpent, which will shortly appear.

The poets descend with Sordello into the hollow. (Dante converses with the judge, Nino Visconti, and with Corrado Malaspina.)

Pointing with his finger, Sordello shews the poets the serpent, appearing through the grass and flowers on the opposite side of the little valley (V. 94-99). The angel, whom Dante can no longer see distinctly through the growing darkness, though he hears the beating of his wings, puts the serpent to flight.

It is possible that the faint and sketchy character of this drawing is a deliberate device of the artist's, indicating the twilight in which the episodes of this Canto are supposed to take place.

The opening line of the Canto appears below, the characters partly effaced:—

S era gia lora che volge el disio
(Era già l'ora che volge il disio).

IX

Overcome by fatigue, Dante falls asleep. He has a vision of an eagle, which, seizing him in its talons, bears him upward to the sphere of purgatorial fire. Awaking, he is informed by Virgil that they are now at the entrance of Purgatory, whither Lucia (the enlightening Grace of Heaven) has conveyed him while he slept. They reach a narrow gate, in front of which are three steps. On the uppermost sits an angel. Instructed by Virgil, Dante falls on his knees before the angel, and implores him to open the gate. The angel, before complying, inscribes seven P's (for *Peccata*, to denote the seven deadly sins from which Purgatory cleanses), with the point of his sword on Dante's forehead. (The close of the Canto, describing the entrance of Dante and Virgil into the first circle of Purgatory, has no illustration.) The first line of the Canto is inscribed in faint characters below the drawing:—

9 la chonchubina di titane anticho
(La concubina di Titone antico).

X

The first circle of Purgatory. After climbing a winding pathway leading through a fissure in the rock, the poets emerge on a flat cornice, running right and left round the mountain, and forming a sort of causeway, the outer edge bordering a sharp declivity, the inner abutting on the precipitous face of the mountain, here of pure white marble, sculptured with skilfully wrought reliefs, illustrating the virtue of humility. The first represents the Annunciation. The second (to the right) David, bringing home the ark on a cart drawn by oxen. His wife Michal gazes contemptuously at the scene from a window of the palace. The third relief represents "The Justice of Trajan". (This episode, taken from the pages of Dion Cassius, was a favourite subject of mediæval art. The legend relates that a poor widow, whose son had been slain, made her complaint to Trajan, just as he was setting forth on a campaign. Notwithstanding his pre-occupations, the Emperor turned about, listened to her case, and caused justice to be administered.)

In the second drawing, the ark and David's palace are lightly sketched in with the silver-point, whereas "The Justice of Trajan", is elaborated into a composition of many figures, very carefully and minutely executed with the pen. It is further distinguished by a peculiar kind of frame. (It is to be observed that the reproduction gives but an inadequate idea of the delicacy and sharpness of the original in this particular instance.)

Dante sees a number of persons approaching, bending under the weight of heavy blocks of stone. These are the proud, who are thus condemned to expiate their sin.

XI

The first circle of Purgatory. The souls of the proud pass along, weighed down by their heavy burdens (cf. Purg. X). Virgil enquires the way of one of them, who reveals himself as Umberto di Santafiore, whose arrogance provoked his countrymen to such a pitch of fury against him, that he was murdered by them at Campagnatico.

Dante recognizes in another the famous miniature painter, Oderisi da Gubbio. Bending to his level, Dante walks along conversing with him: "with equal pace, as oxen in the yoke" (Purg. XII, V. 1).

XII

The first circle of Purgatory. On the floor of the rocky cornice, as on the mountain wall behind it, are various illustrations of fallen pride. Some of these as described in the poem, Botticelli has drawn with the pen, or sketched in silver-point; others he omits altogether. In the foreground to the right, Dante and Virgil contemplate the imagine of the fallen Lucifer (V. 25-27): in the middle distance is shewn Briareus, "with bolt celestial pierced" (V. 28-30); in the background, lightly sketched with the point, the flight of the Assyrians after the death of Holofernes (V. 58-59). To the left of Lucifer, in the foreground, Jupiter, attended by Pallas, Mars and Apollo, contemplates the scattered limbs of the fallen Titans (V. 31-33). Beyond is Nimrod, at the base of the crumbling tower of Babel; Niobe surrounded by the corpses of her children (V. 37-39): and Saul falling upon his sword (the last very slightly sketched). In the corner to the left are seen the ruins of Ilium (V. 60).

Admonished by Virgil, Dante turns to continue the ascent, and encounters an angel, who, clasping him with arms and wings, brings him to a place where steps are hewn in the steep side of the rock. The angel then beats upon Dante's forehead with his wing (V. 98) effacing one of the P's traced there by the angel with the sword. (See the drawing to Canto IX.) Of this Dante becomes aware by touching his forehead as they proceed.

To the left, near the edge of the drawing, two of the proud are still visible, carrying their burdens (cf. Purg. XI).

XIII

Dante and Virgil enter the second circle of Purgatory. Dante sees on this cornice a band of figures in sack-cloth, leaning against the rock, like blind beggars against a church porch. Approaching them, he perceives that their eyes are sewn up with a wire thread. Dante is overcome with pity. They are the envious, who thus expiate their offences. (Dante converses with Sapia, a lady of Siena.)

XIV

Dante and Virgil in the second circle, among the envious, who are represented with sightless eyes seated on the ground, and leaning one against the other (cf. Purg. XIII). To the right of the drawing Dante is shewn conversing with Guido del Duca; beside him sits Rinieri da Calboli. As the poets pass on, they hear voices, resembling the roar of thunder and the hissing of lightning, which record warning instances of envy.

XV

The poets prepare to leave the second circle of Purgatory. Botticelli, taking advantage of Dante's question as to the meaning of Guido del Duca's utterances (V. 43 *et seq.*), again represents the latter, with Rinieri da Calboli beside him, and other groups of the envious in the second circle, though these are no longer present in Canto XV.

A shining apparition confronts Dante, who, dazzled by its splendour, shields his eyes with his hand. It is an angel, who admonishes the poets to continue their ascent.

Botticelli indicates Dante's vision of notable instances of patience, by representing the poet lying asleep on the higher ledge of the mountain.

Dante and Virgil enter the third circle of Purgatory.

XVI

Dante and Virgil in the third circle. Enveloped in a dense mist, they hear the souls of penitents singing the Agnus Dei. The group in the foreground to the left, where Dante catches at the hanging sleeve of Virgil's robe, refers to V. 8-11:

> . . . . . near me drew the faithful guide
> Offering me his shoulder for a stay.
> As the blind man behind his leader walks . . .
> I journey'd through that bitter air and foul.

The singers are the souls of those who have given way to anger. Dante converses with the Lombard, Marco, whose form is concealed from him by the mist.

Strange to say, Botticelli, disregarding the poem, makes the figures distinctly visible, though they are described as shrouded in a dense vapour.

XVII

Dante and Virgil emerge from the thick mist in which the souls of the wrathful are concealed. An angel, still more glorious than the last, appears to conduct them to the fourth circle, which they reach by a flight of steps. A deep stillness reigns on the fourth cornice. It is the circle in which the indolent and indifferent do penance.

XVIII

The fourth circle of Purgatory. Dante moves slowly forward, lost in thought. A hurrying crowd presses on behind him, the shades of those who in life were dilatory and indifferent. Two spirits, the leaders of the band, recount instances of zeal and activity. The scene, as described in the poem, passes by moonlight.

XIX

Dante's vision, described in the opening verses of the Canto, Botticelli indicates as before, by shewing the poet asleep on the ground, and again, by representing him following Virgil, with drooping head, as if absorbed in meditation (V. 40-43).

An angel with outspread wings exhorts the wanderers to continue their ascent. They reach the fifth circle. The souls here imprisoned lie weeping on the ground, their feet and hands bound with fetters, their faces turned to the earth. (They are again represented thus in the two following drawings.) They are the covetous bewailing their sin (V. 115 to 126). Dante converses with Pope Adrian V. Dante sinks upon his knees, in deference to the Papal office, whereupon Adrian bids him rise, declaring that the poet and he are fellow-servants and equals.

XX

The fifth circle of Purgatory. Dante hears a voice extolling the virtue and poverty of Fabricius. Approaching the speaker, he finds him to be Hugh Capet. (They converse together.) Meanwhile, shouts of triumph resound on all sides, and the mountain trembles. Dante and Virgil stand awe-struck for a while, then hastily resume their course.

XXI

The fifth circle of Purgatory. A shade approaches, and explains to the poets that the mountain quakes and the song of joy resounds each time the cleansing of a soul is accomplished. The spirit declares himself to be the poet Statius, and to have just completed his term of penance. On hearing that Virgil stands before him, he attempts to embrace him.

XXII

Dante and Virgil enter the sixth circle of Purgatory with Statius. Dante follows the two poets, who hasten forward, conversing together (V. 7-9). The group of the three poets to the right, below, refers to this episode, while the second group is suggested by the reiterated description of their progress in V. 127-129. Verses 131-134:—

> A tree we found, with goodly fruitage hung
> And pleasant to the smell; and as a fir
> Upward from bough to bough, less ample spreads,
> So downward this less ample spread.

Botticelli has interpreted in the sense of several early commentators, representing the tree with its root above, and its boughs below.

Virgil and Statius approach the tree, from which a voice is heard speaking. Below the drawing are the opening words of the Canto:

gia era lan 22
(Già era l' Angel).

XXIII

Dante, Virgil, and Statius in the sixth circle of Purgatory. While Dante is still gazing into the foliage of the tree, a crowd of spirits approach the wanderers from behind. Pale, hollow-eyed and emaciated, they expiate by hunger and thirst their earthly offence of gluttony. The tree, which has the form of a fir, turned upside down, is laden with perfumed fruits, which excite a desire to eat and drink. Dante recognizes the Florentine Forese among the penitents, and converses with him. (Whereas the tree in the foregoing illustration resembled a fir in growth and foliage, it is here drawn with fruit and leaves like those of the orange-tree.)

XXIV

Dante converses with Forese, who lingers behind the band of spirits. When Forese leaves him, Dante perceives a second tree, and a crowd of spirits, who stretch out their hands to the fruit and foliage. A voice from the tree warns them to desist. The tree is a sapling from the tree of knowledge tasted by Eve, which stands in a higher circle of Purgatory.

The causeway now becomes broader. The three poets move forward, somewhat apart one from another, absorbed in meditation. A shining angel appears to Dante, and points out the way to be followed by those who seek the realms of peace.

In the upper right hand corner of the drawing are shewn the flames of the seventh circle, described in the following Canto.

XXV

Below to the right, only partially carried out, is the group of the three poets, ascending by a cleft in the rocks to the seventh cornice. Dante, who asks how it is possible that spirits, no longer requiring corporeal nourishment, can yet feel hunger and thirst, is referred by Virgil to Statius; the latter explains the phenomenon. They reach the seventh cornice, were the souls of the incontinent are purged by fire from the stain of unlawful love. The strains of the "Summæ Deus Clementiæ" are heard from within the flames.

XXVI

Dante, Virgil and Statius in the seventh circle of Purgatory. The souls of the incontinent do penance in a circle of flame which extends along the cornice, leaving only a narrow space at the outer edge for the passage of the poets. As they are purged in the flames, the spirits sing the praises of chastity.

XXVII

Dante, Virgil and Statius in the seventh circle of Purgatory. Opposing crowds of spirits meet in the flames, and hastily kiss one another. One of the shades remarks the substantiality of Dante's body, and informs him that the bands of spirits running forward in opposite directions are souls doing penance for different degrees of incontinence. The shade then makes himself known as the poet Guido Guinicelli of Bologna.

An angel appears, and commands the poets to follow him through the fire. Dante, clasping his hands, hesitates to obey the order, till admonished by Virgil, and assured that beyond the flames he will once more behold Beatrice. The three poets pass through, Virgil in front, Dante following him, and Statius behind. Emerging from the flames, they begin to ascend steps in the cliff beyond; the sun sets, and the three travellers lie down to rest on the rocks. (Dante's dream.) Virgil resigns his office of conductor, investing Dante "with crown and mitre, sovereign o'er himself," a figure interpreted by Botticelli as the crowning of Dante with a laurel wreath.

XXVIII

Dante, in company with his companions, but no longer conducted by them, enters a pleasant wood at the summit of the mountain of Purgatory. He wanders to the shore of a brook, on the opposite bank of which he sees a beautiful woman, Matilda, gathering flowers, and singing as she walks. At Dante's request she approaches the edge of the brook, the source of the rivers Lethe and Eunoë. (Dante and Matilda converse.)

XXIX

Dante, Virgil and Statius follow Matilda's footsteps, as she advances on the opposite bank of the stream. (Dante sees the wood illumined with supernatural light, and hears sweet music.) A procession approaches, with the triumphal car of the Church in its midst. In front march seven standard-bearers with golden tapers, the flames of which trail behind them on the air, gleaming with the colours of the rainbow, and extending beyond mortal sight. (Symbolic of the seven gifts of the Holy Ghost and the seven Sacraments.) Behind these, four and twenty elders advance in couples. Botticelli represents them with books in their hands, adopting the theory advanced by Landino in his Commentary, that the four and twenty elders typify the books of the Old Testament. The poem describes the elders as crowned with lilies; these, however, Botticelli omits.

The car of the church, which rests on two wheels, is drawn by a Gryphon, the type of Christ. His wings rise high into the air between the streamers of light from the tapers (V. 106-111). Behind the car come the "Three" (the evangelical virtues), then the "Four" (the moral virtues), then an old man, sleeping as he walks (St. John). The car is surrounded by symbols of the four evangelists.

The chariot is only sketched in the drawing. Of the evangelistic symbols only the eagle is carried out with the pen: the six-footed lion is drawn in outline with the silver point. "Three maidens" (Faith, Hope and Charity) dance at the right wheel (V. 121 *et seq.*): "four" (Justice, Valour, Wisdom, Prudence) at the left (V. 130 *et seq.*). St. Paul and St. Luke walk behind the chariot. They are followed by four other old men—"next, four others I beheld of humble seeming". One of these is represented in the drawing as wearing a papal tiara, another with a cardinal's hat, and the remaining two with bishop's mitres. (The figure in the upper corner is sketched in twice; the group of persons immediately following the car is so hastily executed that throughout it is far from distinct.)

The mitres, the cardinal's hat, and the tiara introduced by Botticelli shew that he rejected the current exposition of the text, which identified the "Four" with the Evangelists, in favour of the theory of certain commentators, who saw in these four figures the Fathers of the Church, Ambrose, Augustine, Gregory the Great, and Jerome. (Botticelli's conception is more clearly shewn in the illustration to Canto XXX, where the same group is much more distinctly drawn.)

The Evangelist Saint John follows at a considerable distance from the rest. He is represented asleep, in allusion to his apocalyptic vision. At the edge of the drawing below are the words:—

chantand^{o} 29.

XXX

(The meeting of Dante and Beatrice.) The car is brought to a stand-still; the four and twenty elders, turning to face it, chant "Veni, sponsa de Libano". Angels scatter flowers from above. In the midst of the shower of blossoms Beatrice rises from the car, veiled in white, and crowned with an olive garland. (Dante turns in awe to seek the protection of Virgil; but Virgil has disappeared; Statius stands alone by the Poet's side.) Beatrice impressively rebukes Dante.

Between Dante and the triumphal procession with its car lies the brook Eunoë. The allegorical figures of the four moral virtues dance beside the left wheel of the chariot, behind which stand St. Paul, and St. Luke, the four Fathers, and the slumbering St. John (cf. Purg. XXIX). The Gryphon's wings rise between the streaming banderoles of light that flow from the tapers, in such a manner that the central streamer floats between the wings (Purg. XXIV, V. 109-111). (Landino in his Commentary explains this central streamer to typify the Sacrament of the Eucharist.)

XXXI

The procession remains stationary. Beatrice addresses Dante, rebuking him for certain offences.

Botticelli's drawing deals more especially with the objects described in V. 92-133.

Matilda now seizes Dante, and draws him through the water towards the opposite bank, the stream immersing him to the chin, while his conductress skims across the waves, "swift as a shuttle". She finally dips his head under the water (V. 101).

> . . . . thence raising up
> Within the fourfold dance of lovely nymphs
> Presented me so laved; and with their arms
> They each did cover me. (V. 103-105.)

The four maidens lead Dante to the Gryphon's breast (V. 113), "where, turn'd toward us, Beatrice stood" (V. 114). Botticelli, however, disregarding the words of the poet, depicts her still seated in the chariot, and addressing Dante, round whom are grouped the four nymphs, from this eminence.

The three theological virtues then advance, dancing and singing (V. 131-132). (They beg Beatrice to remove her veil.)

In accordance with the text, Botticelli has made the scenery of his drawing the same, in all essentials, as that of the illustrations to Cantos XXIX and XXX. In the centre is the car, with the Gryphon, whose wings rise up through the streaks of light. The chariot is surrounded by the symbols of the four Evangelists; behind it are the "Seven" (St. Paul and St. Luke, the four Fathers, and the Evangelist St. John). A few of the four and twenty elders, who march before the car, holding books in their out-stretched hands, are still visible in the left-hand corner of the drawing.

XXXII

Dante sees the chariot turn suddenly to the right. He follows at the left wheel, with Statius and Matilda. They come to the tree of the knowledge of good and evil, where Beatrice quits the chariot. She seats herself on the ground at the root of the tree, the seven bearers of the tapers surrounding her (V. 85 *et seq.*). The Gryphon binds the pole of the chariot to the tree (V. 96).

The chariot undergoes a transformation as Dante gazes at it. An eagle appears in the tree, swoops down into the car, and leaves it "lined with his feathers". A dragon comes out from between the wheels, while on every part of the car monstrous heads spring forth, three, horned like oxen, on the pole; one, with a single horn on the brow, at each corner. A harlot guarded by a giant who embraces her, stands upon it. (An allegory on the state of the church.)

The elders are seen disappearing among the streamers of light above (V. 17-18).

The figures of Dante and Statius re-appear several times among the various groups.

XXXIII

(At the close of the thirty-second canto the desecrated car, with the giant and the harlot, disappears into the depths of the forest.)

Beatrice still remains seated at the root of the tree, surrounded by the "Three", and the "Four". The seven maidens chant a hymn. At Beatrice's command they then continue their course. (Beatrice and Dante converse as they walk.) They come to a fountain, on the summit of Purgatory, the source of Lethe and Eunoë. At Beatrice's command, Matilda leads Dante, accompanied by Statius, to drink of the waters of Eunoë. Refreshed and strengthened by the heavenly draught, Dante is prepared for his entrance into Paradise:—

Pure and made apt for mounting to the stars. (V. 145.)

PARADISO

I

In the illustrations to this canto, Botticelli shews us Dante conducted by Beatrice to the spheres of Paradise. They are depicted floating upwards over meadows watered by the stream of Eunoë. The artist has drawn his inspiration from the closing verse of the Purgatorio: —

Pure and made apt for mounting to the stars,

from V. 47 and 48 of Canto I of the Paradiso, which describe Beatrice as gazing upwards at the sun, like the eagle, and from the imagery of verses 92, 93, 136-139, illustrating the lightning-course of Dante and his mistress through the air, a course which, governed by the natural laws of the sphere they have entered, has become so swift and easy as to be almost imperceptible to the poet. (Cf. also Par. II. 22: "Beatrice upward gazed, and I on her.")

II

Dante's discourse with Beatrice, in the sphere of the moon, entering which they seem to be enveloped in a cloud of diamond. The drawing is suggested by V. 127-136:

The virtue and motion of the sacred orbs
As mallet by the workman's hands, must needs
By blessed movers be inspired. This heaven
Made beauteous by so many luminaries,
From the deep spirit that moves its circling sphere,
Its image takes, an impress like a seal.
And as the soul that dwells within your dust,
Through members different, yet together form'd,
In different power resolves itself: e'en so
The intellectual efficacy unfolds
Its goodness multiplied throughout the stars.

III

Dante and Beatrice in the sphere of the moon. Dante sees forms shining faintly through the luminous atmosphere, and takes them for reflections of actual substances. He looks first backwards, then forwards in search of their supposed originals, an action the artist suggests by drawing the poet's head in both attitudes. Beatrice explains to Dante that the forms he mistakes for reflections are the souls of those who have involuntarily broken their vows.

> Straight to the shadow which for converse seem'd
> Most earnest, I address'd me . . . (V. 34, 35.)

This was the nun, Piccarda. Dante converses with her.

IV

Dante and Beatrice in the sphere of the moon. The souls of the blessed float around them in space (cf. Par. III). Beatrice reads in Dante's face the doubts that perplex his mind, and answers the questions he would fain propound, as to whether the good intentions of one person can be annulled by the violence of another, and as to the correctness of Plato's theory, that the souls of men return, after death on earth, to their appointed stars in the heavens.

V

As Dante gazes on Beatrice, he is dazzled by the supernatural brightness of her face. (Close of Canto IV.) She answers Dante's enquiry, as to whether man by other service can make atonement for broken vows in the negative.

VI

The second part of the fifth canto relates how Dante and Beatrice ascend to the sphere of the second planet, Mercury. Botticelli's next drawing seems to have been inspired by V. 91 *et seq.* in Canto V:

> And as the arrow, ere the cord is still
> Leapeth unto its mark, so on we sped
> Into the second realm. There I beheld
> The dame so joyous enter that the orb
> Grew brighter at her smiles . . .

Dante sees thousands of shining spirits flashing through the air like fish in a lake. The sixth canto, being mainly occupied with the discourse between Dante and the Emperor Justinian, offered no special incidents for pictorial treatment.

VII

Dante and Beatrice linger in Mercury, surrounded by troops of shining spirits. Other doubts arise in Dante's mind. He discourses of them with Beatrice.

VIII

Dante and Beatrice enter the third heaven, the sphere of the planet Venus. Glorified spirits circle round them in rapid flight. (Dante converses with Charles Martel, son of Charles II of Naples.)

IX

Dante and Beatrice in the sphere of Venus. (Another resplendent soul approaches the poet.) The drawing probably refers to V. 16 *et seq.*

> . . . . The eyes
> Of Beatrice, resting as before
> Firmly upon me, manifested forth
> Approval of my wish.

X

Dante and Beatrice enter the sphere of the sun. The drawing illustrates V. 52-59:

> And thus to me Beatrice: "Thank, oh thank
> The Sun of Angels, him, who by his grace
> To this perceptible hath lifted thee."
> Never was heart in such devotion bound
> And with complacency so absolute
> Disposed to render up itself to God
> As mine was at those words.

XI

Dante and Beatrice in the sphere of the Sun. The design of this drawing, which, like the next in order, may have been only partially

10

carried out, seems to have been suggested to Botticelli by the opening lines of Canto XI, in which Dante expresses his sense of happiness at having been withdrawn from the trivialities of human life to be the guest of Heaven with Beatrice (V. 1-12). Dante's gesture apparently expresses some such thought. (Thomas Aquinas converses with Dante.)

XII

Dante and Beatrice in the sphere of the Sun. Botticelli no doubt intended to carry out this design in much greater detail; only the figures of Dante and Beatrice were completed, however. Dante finds himself surrounded by two circles of glorified souls, which he likens to a double rainbow. (The Franciscan, Buonaventura, celebrates the virtues of Saint Dominic.)

XIII

Dante and Beatrice in the sphere of the Sun. The twin rainbows circle in opposite courses round Dante (cf. Par. XI and XII). Thomas Aquinas resumes his converse with Dante.

XIV

This drawing deals with the second part of Canto XIV (from V. 67). Dante and Beatrice ascend to a higher sphere, that of Mars. In the mien and gestures of the poet, Botticelli endeavours to express Dante's awe and rapture on beholding the vision of beatific light, and hearing the hymns of praise sung to Christ by glorified spirits.

XV

Dante and Beatrice in the sphere of Mars. Dante notes with amazement the apparition of a luminous form, which darts forward from out the clustered spirits. It is the spirit of his ancestor, Cacciaguida. (Cacciaguida tells the history of his own life, and of the Florence of his times.)

XVI

Dante and Beatrice in the sphere of Mars. A feeling of pride in his ancestry rises in Dante's heart as he listens to Cacciaguida's tale. Beatrice, smiling a gentle rebuke, stands somewhat apart. Botticelli has chosen this episode for his text. (Cacciaguida continues his account of Florence and her ancient clans.)

XVII

Dante and Beatrice in the sphere of Mars. They continue to talk with Cacciaguida. Dante longs to learn what his own future will be from Cacciaguida. Beatrice encourages him to express his wish. (Cacciaguida describes the future fate of Dante.)

XVIII

Dante and Beatrice ascend to the sixth sphere, that of Jupiter. The half seen figures of Dante and Beatrice rising over the lower boundary of the circle, by which the sixth sphere is denoted, illustrate the text with great felicity:—

> Vanquishing me with a beam
> Of her soft smile, she spake: "Turn thee, and list.
> These eyes are not thine only Paradise."

At the bottom of the page are the opening words of the canto, partly cut off:—

18 gia si ghodeuaso . .
(Già si godeva solo).

XIX

Dante and Beatrice in the sphere of Jupiter. (The flaming eagle discourses to Dante of unjust rulers contemporary with the poet.)

This drawing is less finished than the last.

XX

Dante and Beatrice in the sphere of Jupiter. Dante listens to the hymns of the blessed, and to the further speech of the flaming eagle.

Below are the opening words of the canto:—

quando cholui 20
(Quando colui).

XXI

Dante and Beatrice ascend to the seventh heavenly sphere, that of Saturn. Beatrice no longer smiles on Dante as before, for her loveliness, increasing in each new sphere, is such as the poet's mortal eyes could no longer bear to contemplate in its full intensity (V. 1-12). This is the idea suggested by the artist in the earnest gravity of Beatrice's expression, as she turns to Dante. The poet sees a ladder, so lofty that its top is out of sight; upon its steps throng a multitude of shining spirits, flocking and wheeling past each other "like crows at day-break". The spirits are represented in the form of winged genii, fluttering in brilliant circles in and out between the steps of the ladder. On the upper part of the ladder the figure of Dante re-appears, floating on the arm of Beatrice, who points upwards. This group, when nearly completed, was partially erased, probably by the artist himself; enough remains, however, to make the figures recognizable. There is no description of the ascent in Canto XXI, but we may conclude that Botticelli intended to draw upon the following canto for the enrichment of his design, and that he afterwards abandoned the idea (cf. the corresponding illustration to Canto XXII).

XXII

The closing verses of Canto XXI relate how Dante is deafened by a sudden shout.

The lower group in this drawing illustrates V. 1-7:

> Astounded, to the guardian of my steps
> I turn'd me, like the child, who always runs
> Thither for succour, where he trusteth most.
> And she was like the mother, who her son
> Beholding pale and breathless, with her voice
> Soothes him, and he is cheer'd; for thus she spake,
> Soothing me: "Knowst thou not, thou art in Heaven?"

Beatrice explains the shout as a cry for vengeance, and draws Dante after her up the ladder (V. 100-101). They ascend in rapid flight to the eighth heaven, the sphere of the fixed stars. (Beatrice commands Dante to look downward through the seven spheres, and estimate the distance he has travelled from the earth, which moves him to a smile by the insignificance of its appearance from that height.)

XXIII

Dante and Beatrice in the sphere of the fixed stars. Thousands of blessed spirits circle round the light of Christ, who shines in their midst like the sun at noon-day (V. 94 *et seq.*). Botticelli has dwelt only upon this, among the varied phenomena described by the poet. The constellations of the Twins and the Bull are lightly sketched with the silver point, under the feet of Dante and Beatrice (cf. Par. XXII, V. 110-111).

XXIV

Dante and Beatrice in the sphere of the fixed stars. Christ shines like the sun at noon-day. The souls of the blessed revolve round this sun, from which they receive their light, as around a fixed pole (cf. Par. XXIII). The drawing seems to refer more especially to the opening verses of the canto, in which Beatrice begs the blessed spirits to satisfy Dante's thirst for heavenly knowledge.

The glowing light which envelopes the soul of St. Peter hovers over the heads of Dante and Beatrice. On it is inscribed the name: "Piero".

XXV

Dante and Beatrice in the sphere of the fixed stars. The holy fires circle round Christ, the Sun. After St. Peter's colloquy with Dante, another light detaches itself from the galaxy, and advances towards him. This is St. James the Apostle. Beatrice addresses Dante (V. 17-18):

> "Lo! lo! behold the peer of mickle might
> That makes Galicia throng'd with visitants."

(Alluding to Compostella in Galicia, the shrine of St. James.) The composition is suggested by these lines.

Three flames, inscribed respectively "Piero", "Giovanni", "Jachopo", hover over Dante's head.

XXVI

Dante and Beatrice in the sphere of the fixed stars (cf. the last drawing). Dante is so dazzled by the glory of St. John, that he loses the power of sight for a while. The illustration, however, seems to deal, not with this episode, but with the description in V. 70-76. Dante, having concluded the speech in which he discourses of the effects of man's love for God, recovers his sight.

> And as a sleep is broken and dispersed
> Through sharp encounter of the nimble light
> With the eye's spirit running forth to meet
> The ray, from membrane on to membrane urg'd,
> And the upstartled wight loathes that he sees;
> So, at his sudden waking, he misdeems
> Of all around him, till assurance waits
> On better judgment; thus the saintly dame
> Drove from before mine eyes the motes away.

(Beatrice tells him that the fourth light, which now approaches him, is Adam, the father of mankind.)

Over the heads of Dante and Beatrice are four lights, inscribed respectively: "Piero", "Giovanni", "Jachopo", "Adamo".

XXVII

Dante and Beatrice linger in the heaven of the fixed stars. Peter speaks with indignation of the actual state of the church.

The holy flames then vanish upwards. Beatrice exhorts Dante to cast his eyes down once more, and note the distance he has travelled since his last observation (Par. XXII). Dante sees the tract he has passed over, and a portion of the earth illuminated by the sun. Dante and Beatrice then ascend from the constellation Gemini (Castor and Pollux, "Leda's children", V. 98), to the ninth, or highest heaven.

XXVIII

Dante and Beatrice in the ninth heaven (the Primum Mobile). Dante sees a point of intense light, encompassed by nine successive rings of flame, which circle swiftly round it, those nearest the central point being the most brilliant. Beatrice explains the phenomenon; the nine circles are the angelic orders, the central light is the divine essence. The angels are divided into three hierarchies (one to each Person of the Blessed Trinity): which hierarchies are subdivided each into three orders. The hierarchy nearest to the divine essence consists of Cherubim, Seraphim, and Thrones; these are succeeded by the second hierarchy, Dominations, Virtues, and Powers; and finally, by the three inferior orders, Principalities, Archangels, and Angels.

Botticelli, influenced, very probably, by the descriptions of the hierarchies and orders given by Dante in the "Convito" (II 6), where their titles differ somewhat from those assigned them in the Divina Commedia, has attempted to distinguish them by various attributes. Thus, his angels of the first hierarchy, which the "Convito" explains as typifying the omnipotence of God the Father, are provided with rings (symbols of the universe?), shields, and banners. In the second hierarchy, which typifies the wisdom of the Saviour, Botticelli depicts the angels of the first order with apples and rods in their hands, alluding, perhaps, to Christ's dominion in the world. The attributes of the remaining orders are less easily distinguishable. (The third hierarchy corresponds to the gifts of the Holy Ghost.)

In the centre of the drawing we see Dante, lost in contemplation of the angelic vision. Beatrice, standing beside him, points upwards.

One of the angels in the lowest circle holds a cartellino, on which is inscribed in minute characters the name of the artist: Sandro di Mariano. (Cf. p. 17.)

On the extreme edge of the sheet of vellum, to the right, the names of the various orders are inscribed in Botticelli's own hand. When the sheet was cut, the final letters of the words came away. The inscription, as it now stands, is as follows. At the top, indicating the seat of the Godhead, is the word trinit(a), then:

cherub(ini)
serafi(ni)
tron(i)
domin(azioni)
virtut(es)
podest(adi)
princ(ipati)
arch(angeli)
ang(eli).

XXIX

Dante and Beatrice in the ninth, or highest sphere, the angelic orders circling round the divine essence. Beatrice instructs Dante concerning the manner of creation, nature, and number of the angels.

XXX

Dante and Beatrice ascend to the Empyrean, the heaven of pure light. The drawing is based chiefly on V. 61 *et seq.* Dante sees a river of light, the banks of which are radiant with miraculous flowers; "living sparks", which the artist represents by winged genii, fly from the waters of the stream, and dip into the cups of the flowers; then, as if drunk with perfume, plunge again into the tide. As one sinks under the waves, another rises.

XXXI

No drawing to this canto.

XXXII

At the close of the thirtieth canto, the poet's vision of the hosts of the blessed under the figure of a heavenly rose of immeasurable size, is described. Beatrice now leaves him, to take her place in the mystic rose, and St. Bernard appears at Dante's side in her stead. The same image governs the structure of the two final cantos. The design for Canto XXXII, which was evidently destined to include a large number of figures, was never completed. The only figures drawn with the pen are the small sketches of Christ and the Virgin. The composition is suggested by Par. XXXI. V. 115 *et seq.*

> . . . Search around
> The circles to the furthest, till thou spy
> Seated in state, the queen that of this realm
> Is sov'ran.

The floating figure is probably meant for the Angel Gabriel. (V. 112 -113.)

The last two sheets are blank.

PLATES

The reproductions, with the exception of Plate XXXIV*a* in the Inferno series, are exactly half the size of the originals.

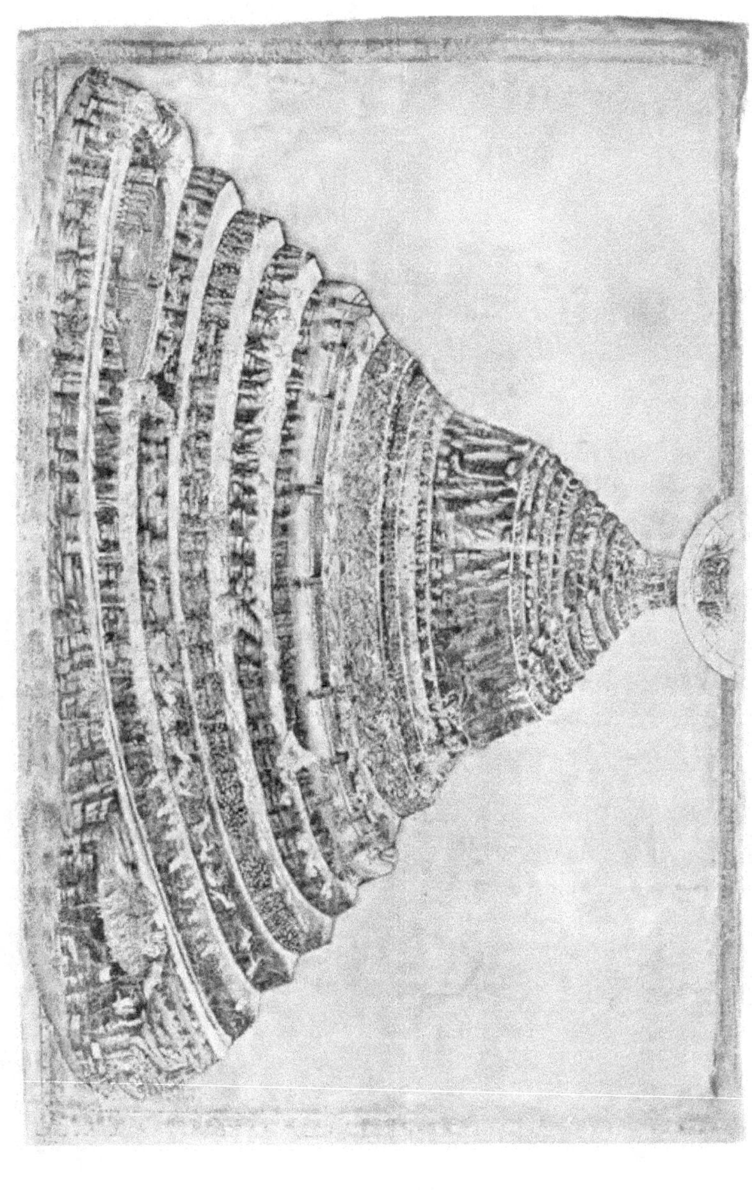

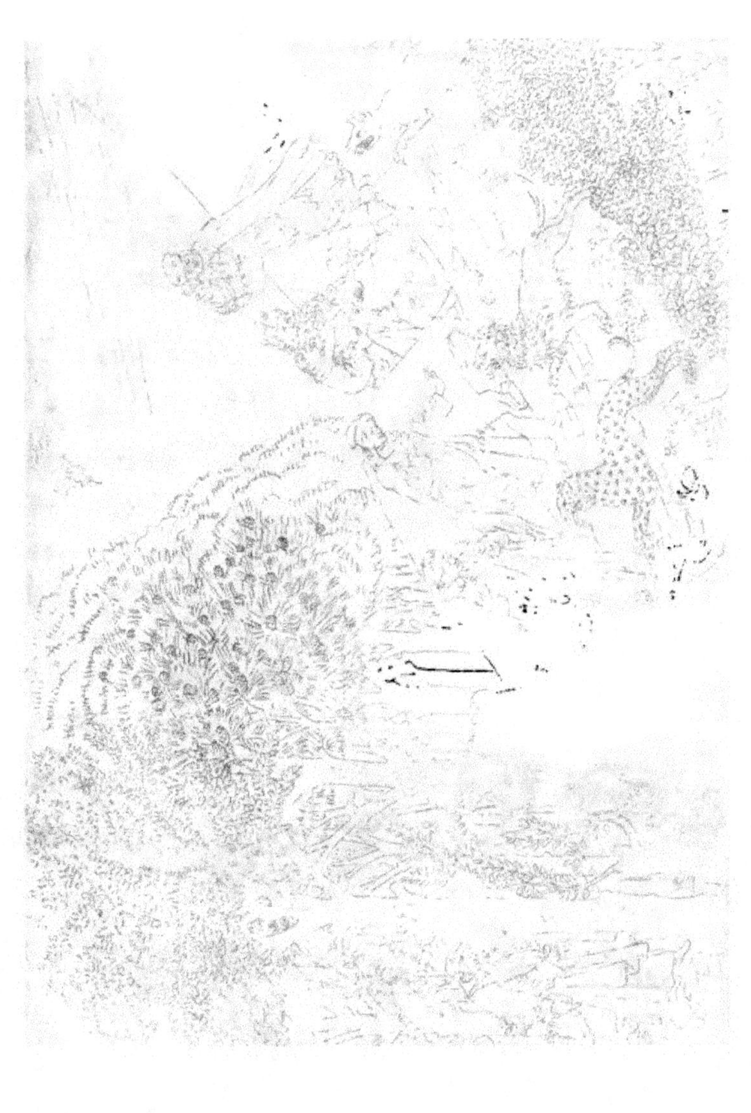

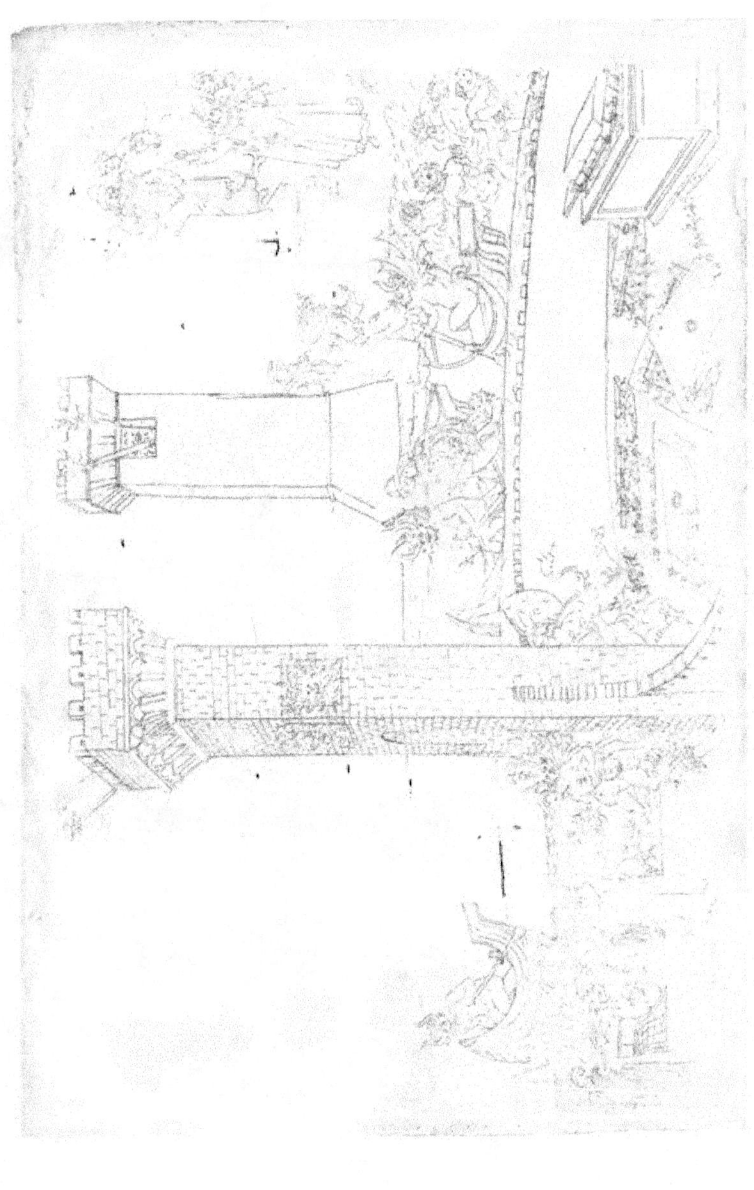

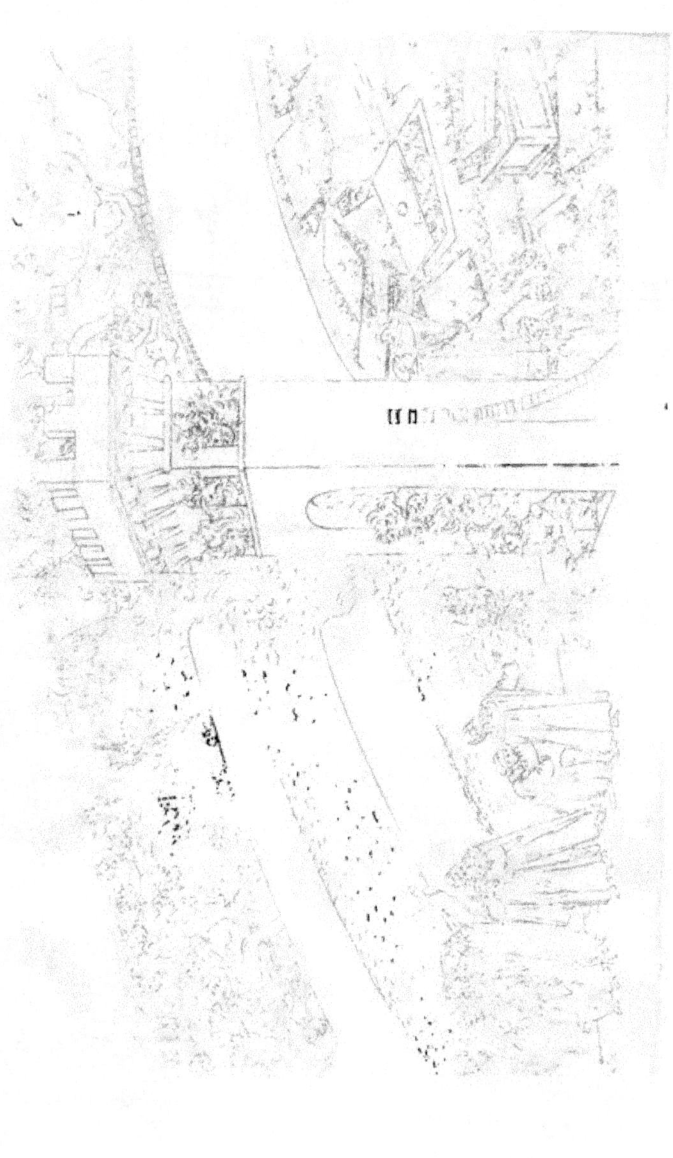

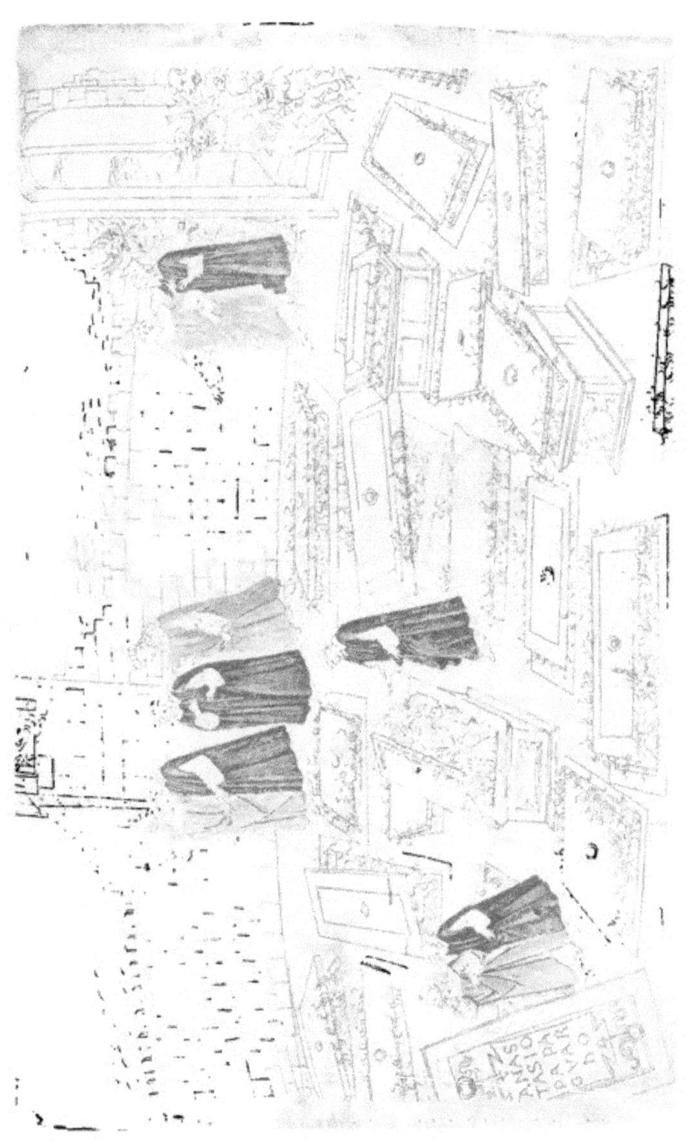

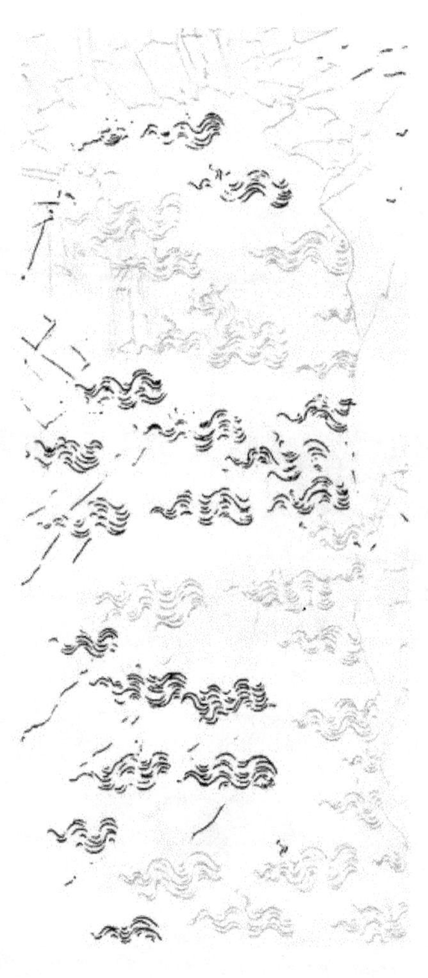

INFERNO XXX

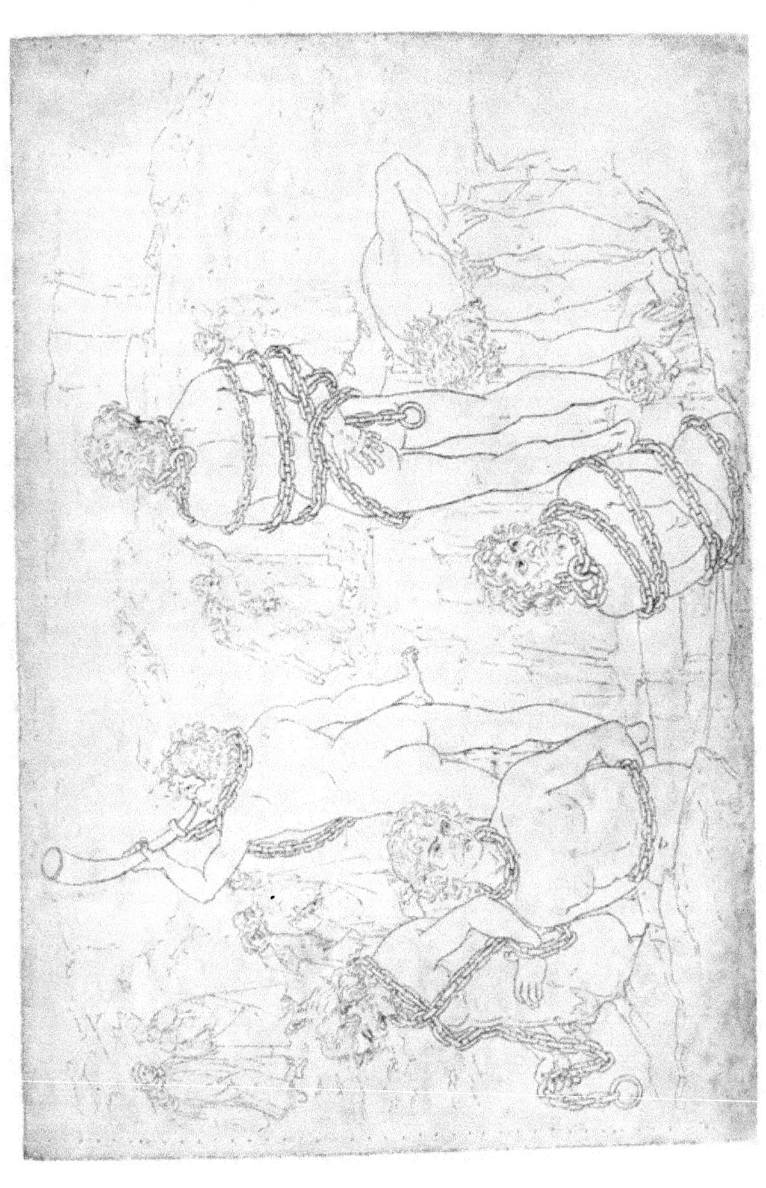

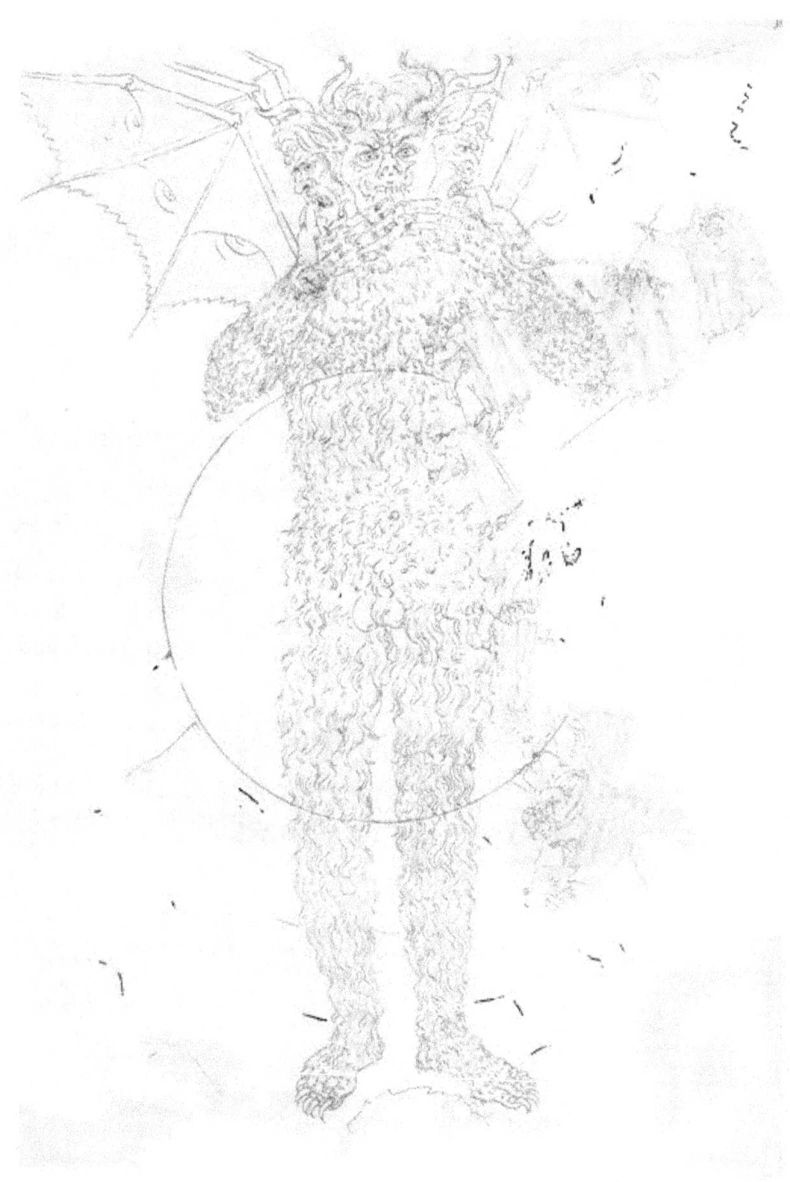

INFERNO XXXIV

PURGATORIO VI

PURGATORIO VIII

PURGATORIO XVI

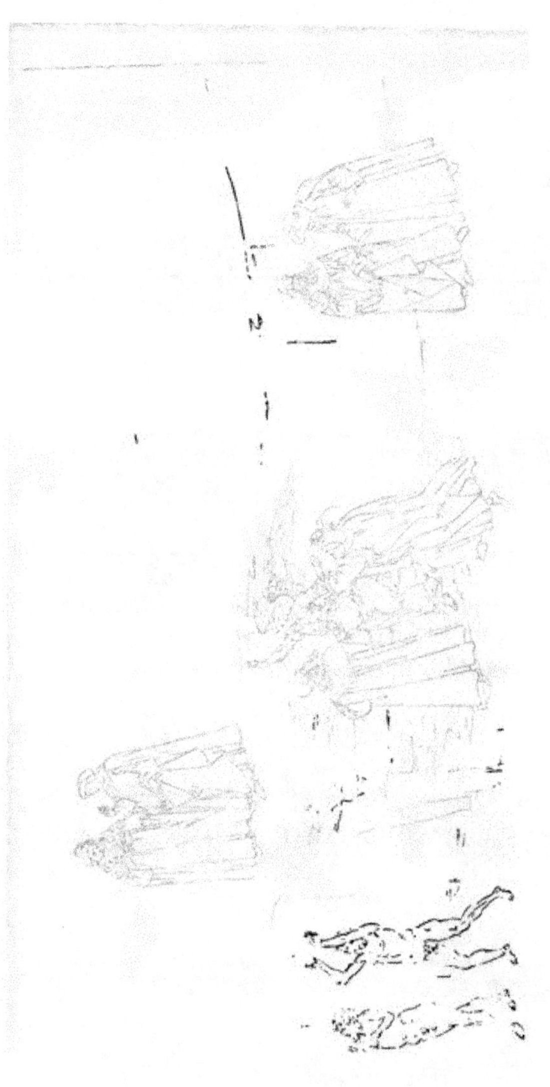

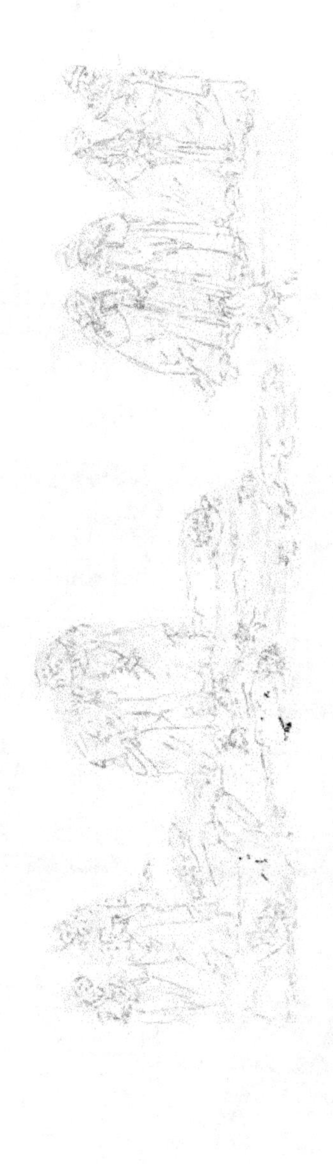

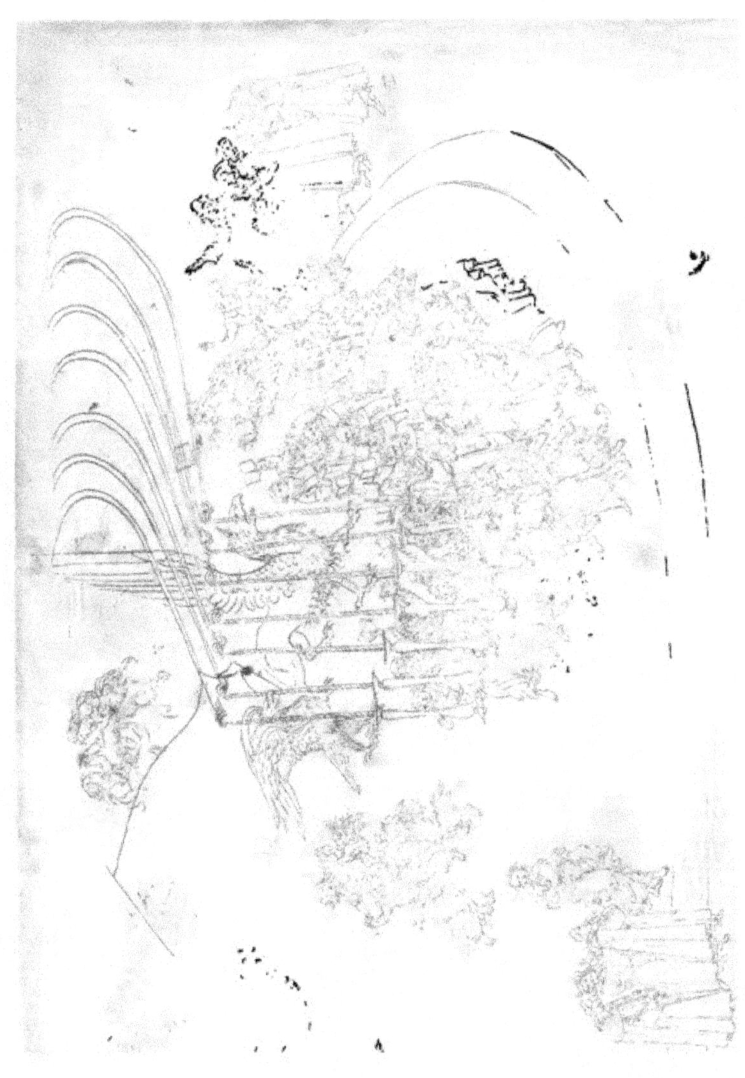

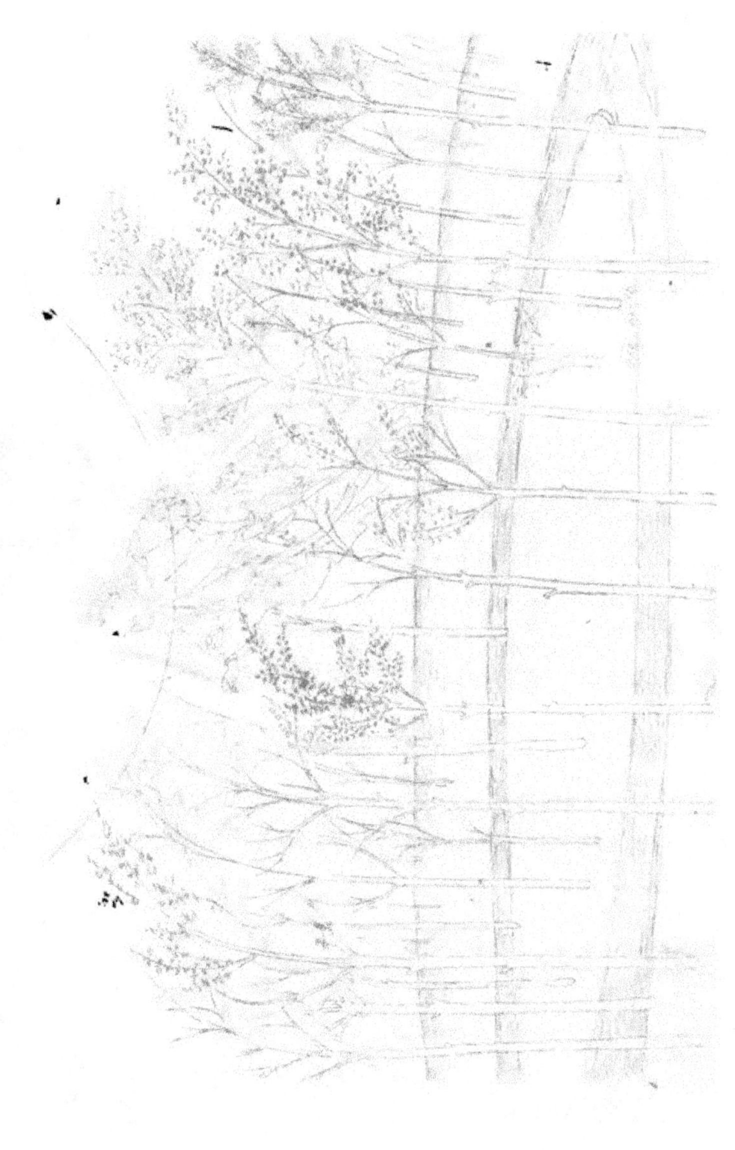

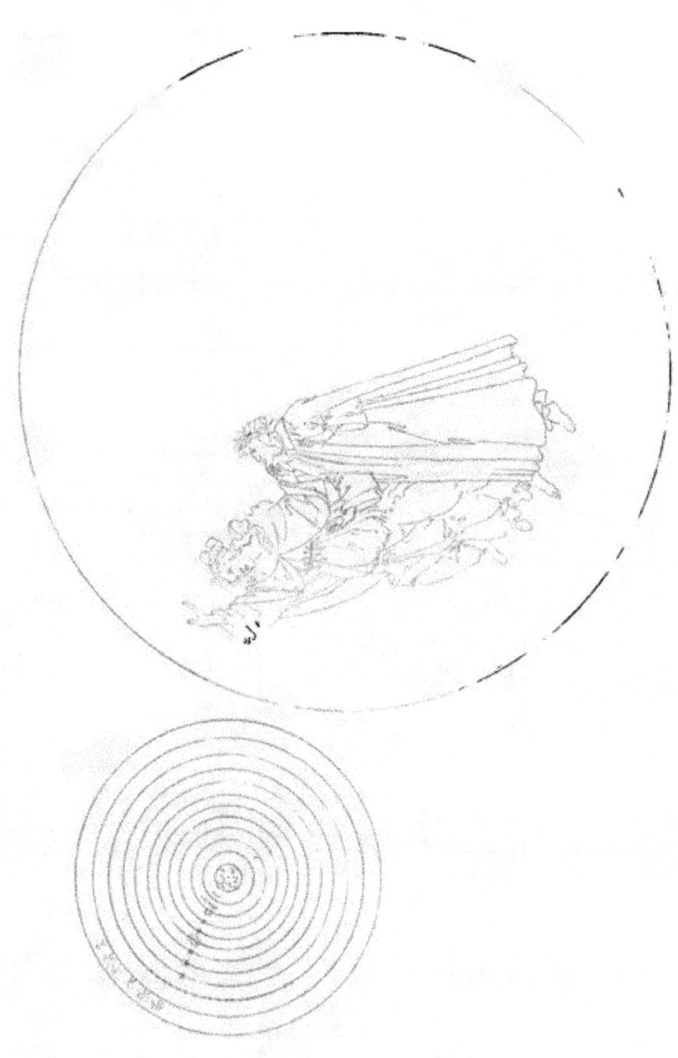

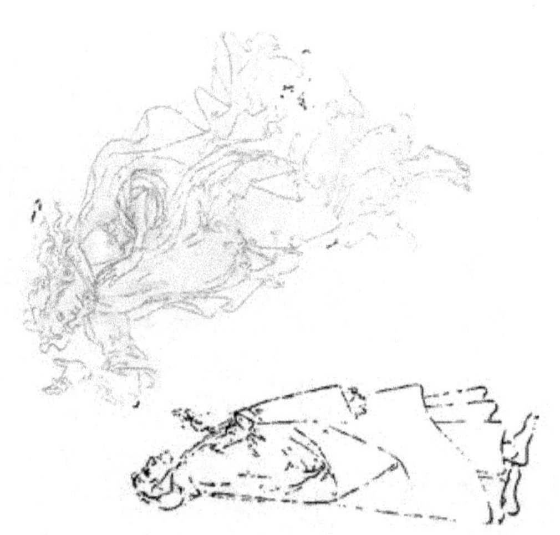

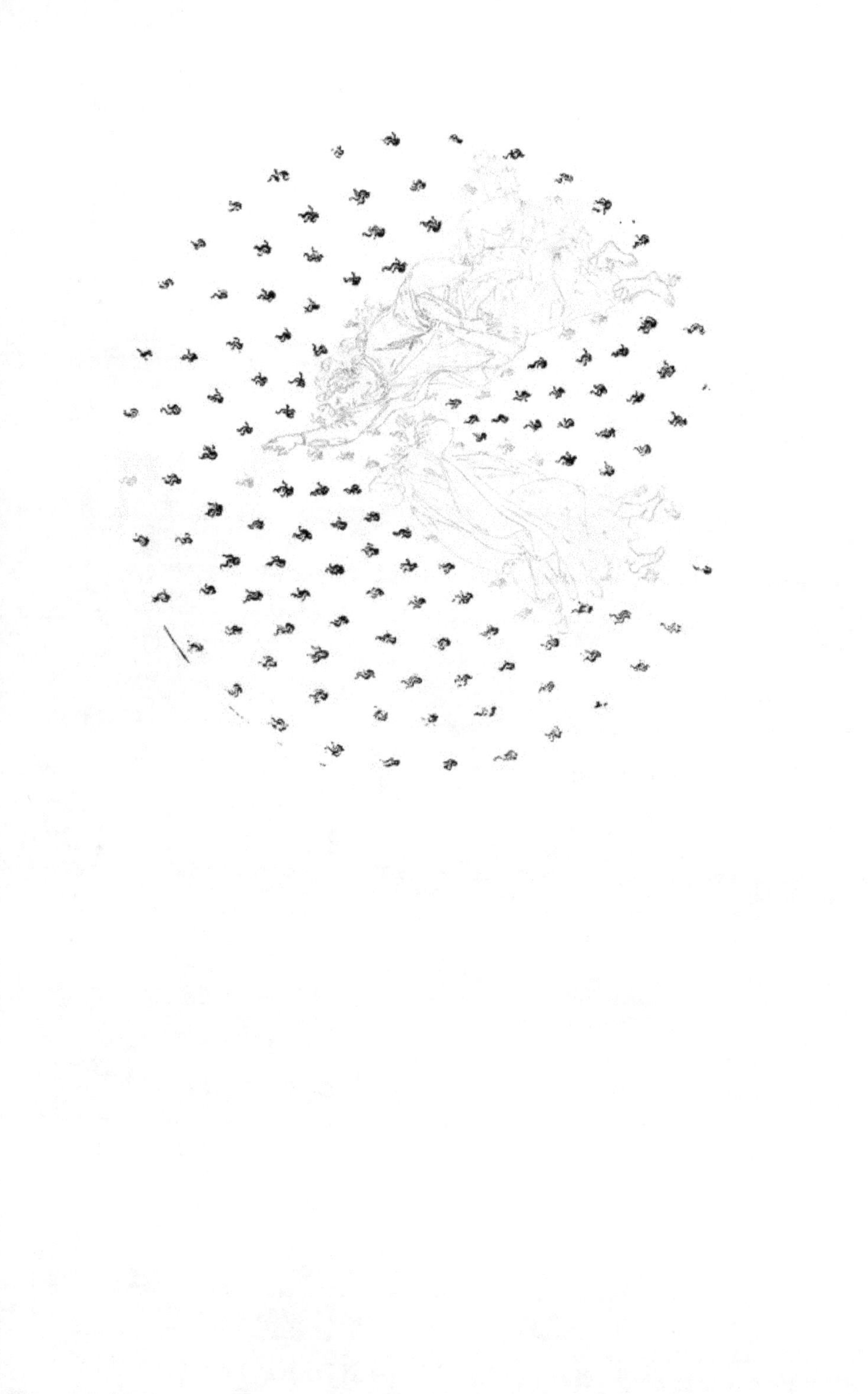

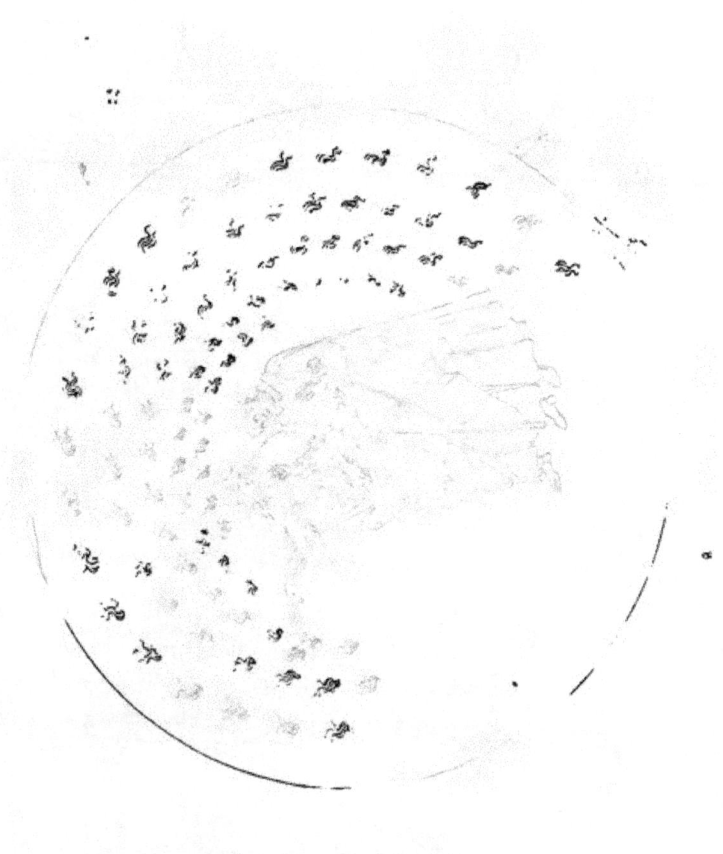

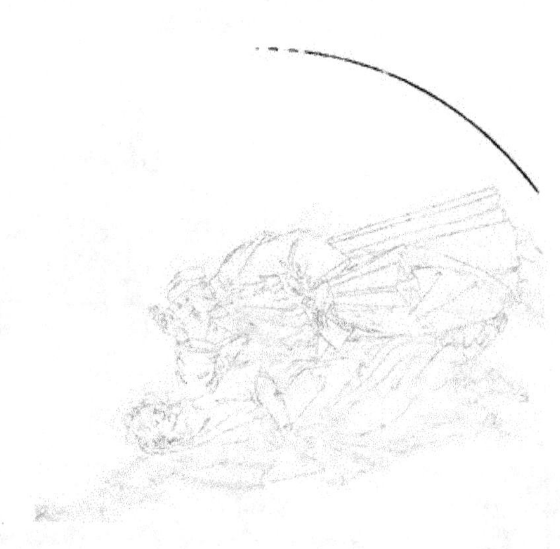

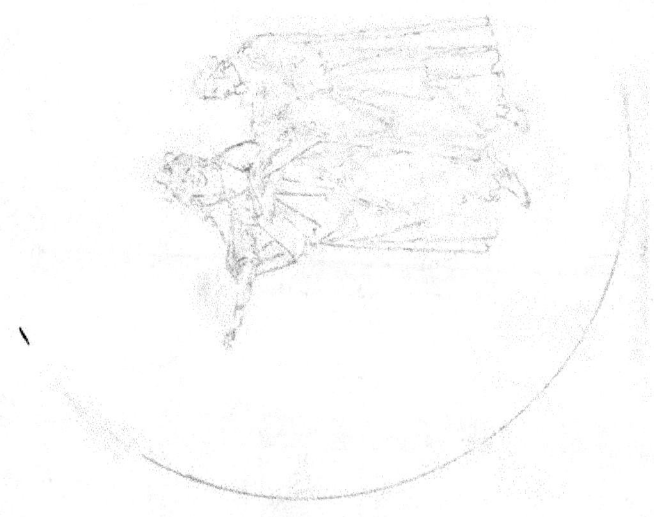

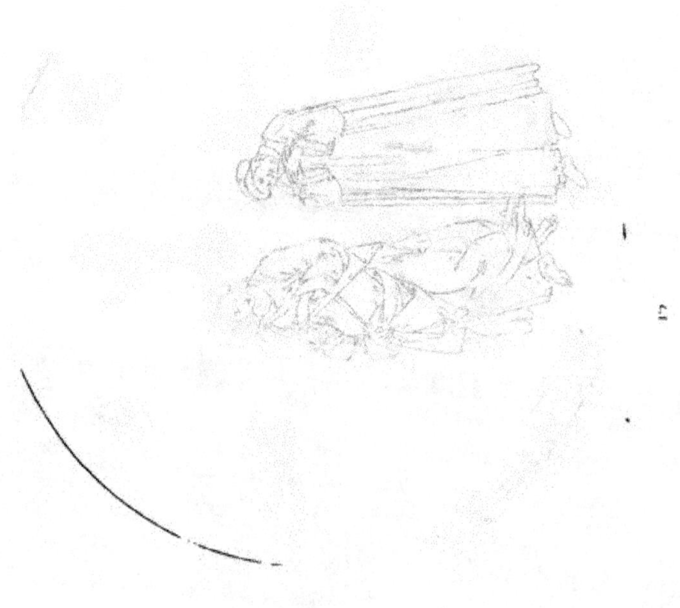

17

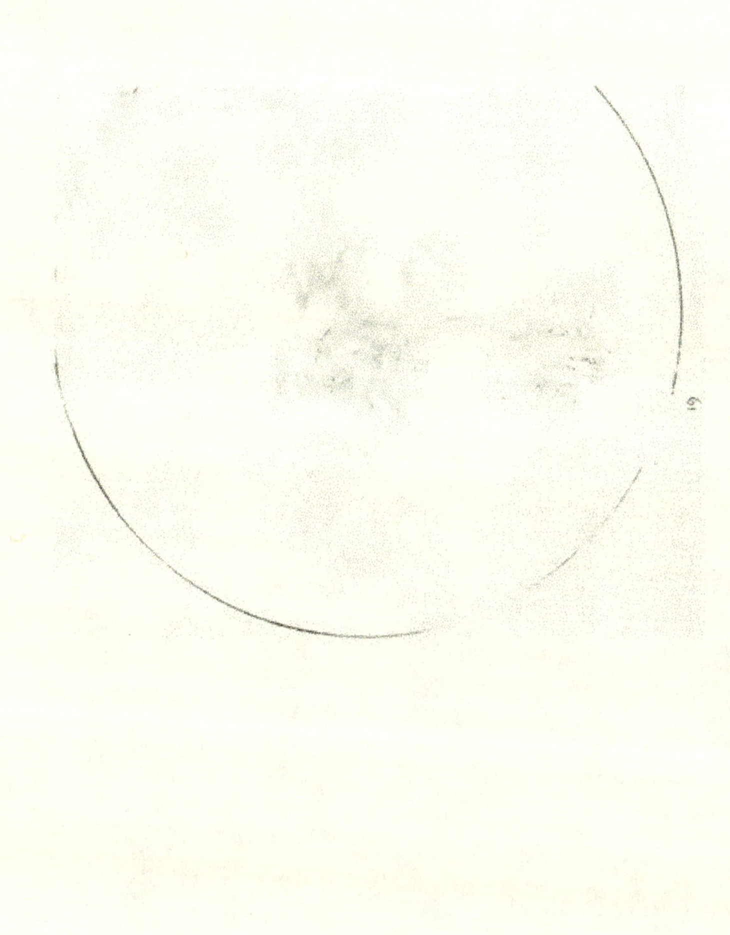

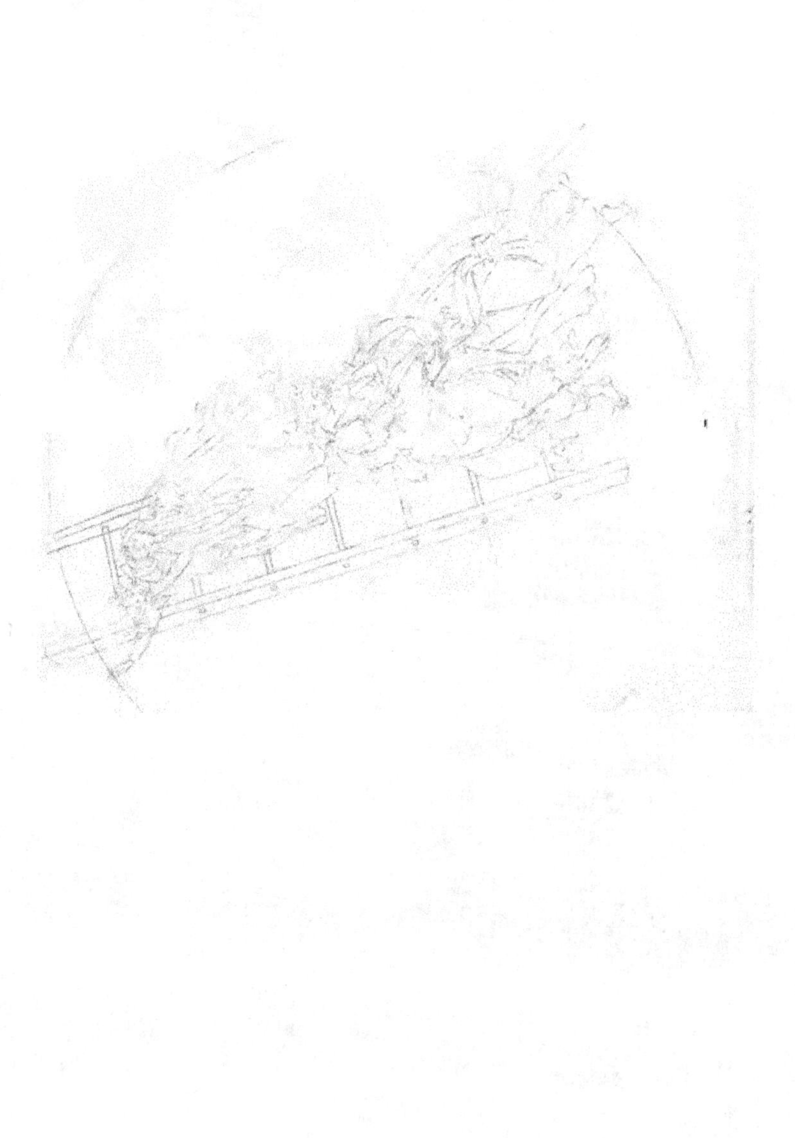

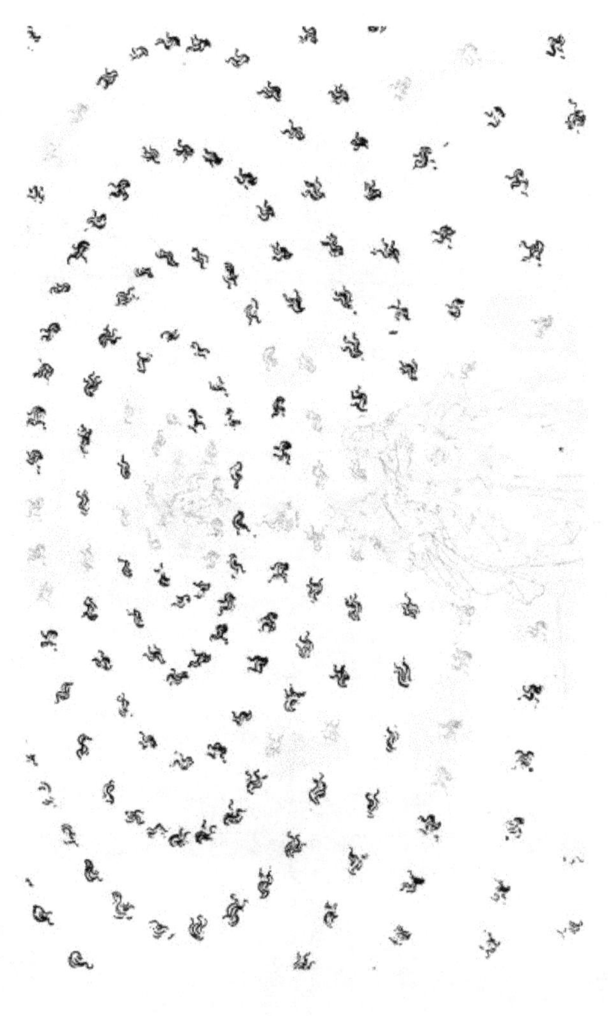

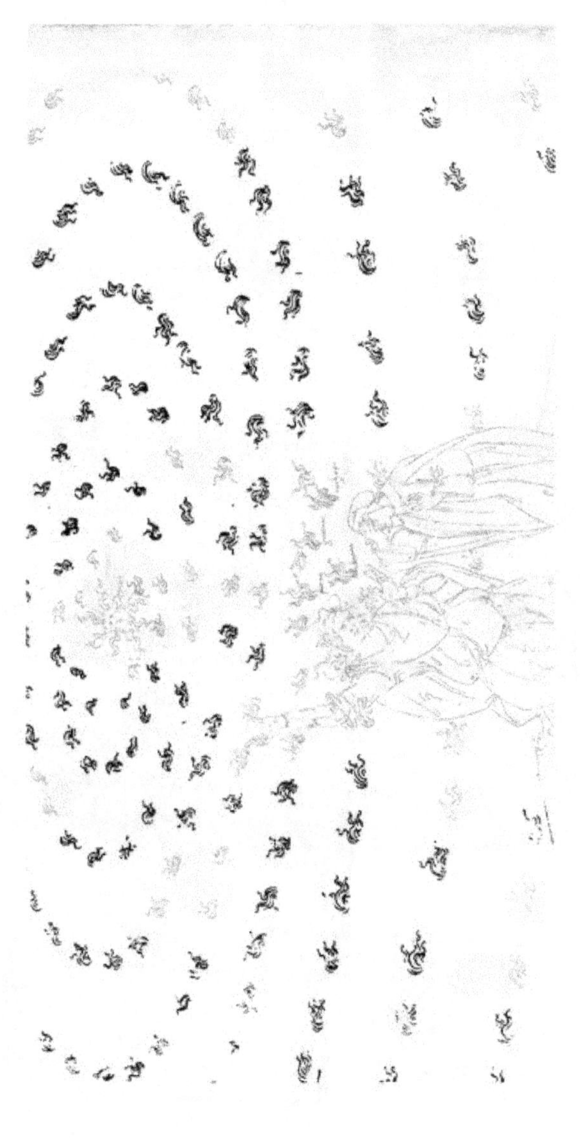

www.ingramcontent.com/pod-product-compliance
Lightning Source LLC
Chambersburg PA
CBHW030348270326
41926CB00009B/1007

* 9 7 8 3 3 3 7 2 4 6 0 9 9 *